# HAUNTED
## LIVERPOOL 1

For Daniel Moss of E Rex Makin & Co.



Published by The Bluecoat Press, Liverpool
Book design by MARCH Graphic Design Studio, Liverpool
Front cover illustration by Peter Whitfield
Printed by Ashford Colour Press

ISBN 1 872568 53 X

Tom Slemen

# HAUNTED LIVERPOOL 1

The Bluecoat Press

# Contents

# How my Interest Began

My interest in ghosts started when I was a child, when my mother told me about a ghost she had seen in the mid-1970s. At the time, we lived in a house in Myrtle Street. One night my mother was in the kitchen when she noticed a figure moving quickly towards the hall. She presumed it was my sister, but when she went to her bedroom to check, my sister was sound asleep.

Later that night, she got into bed and was about to drop off to sleep when she heard footsteps approaching. A stout woman, dressed like a Victorian maid, came through the wall carrying a platter with a cover over it. My mother said that she heard the rustle of the maid's skirts as she went by. The ghost walked through the bottom of the bed – and through her legs and, as the figure passed through the wall at the corner of the room, she heard the sound of children cheering.

As soon as the figure vanished through the wall, the sounds stopped. Mum did not tell anyone about the ghostly encounter but, a week later, a neighbour told her she was moving because she had seen the ghosts of young boys standing in her bedroom. They always came from the same point in the room and mum told her that on the other side of the wall was the exact spot in her bedroom where the ghostly maid had vanished.

Years later, I found an old map of Edge Hill and was surprised to see that an orphanage had stood on the site of our old house in Victorian times and that the kitchen was in the exact same space as the bedroom of our house and our neighbour's. And so my interest in ghosts began ...

# Introduction

In 1875, the Director of the American Patent Office sent his resignation to the Secretary of the Board of Trade. His reason for resigning was simple; he said he was quitting because, "there was nothing left to invent".

This false sense of security is fostered by the notion that we are living in an age of technological marvels. However, when we compare the little that we do know with all that we do not, it becomes clear that man inhabits a world where maps and scientific theories are still incomplete; a world where people, ships and planes can still disappear without trace. There is so much on this earth that is unknown to man and only a fool, or devoted sceptic, can fail to realise this.

Many freethinkers throughout the ages have dared to confront the unknown head-on, even in the face of ridicule. In the long history of human stupidity there have been many who have steered us from ignorance and superstition: Nicolas Copernicus (1473–1543); Galileo Galilei (1564–1642); Charles Darwin (1809–1892); Sigmund Freud (1856–1939); and Louis Pasteur (1822–1895). All these people and their inventions were hooted and howled at in their day. Entrenched authority has always opposed new concepts, so the contents of this book you are about to read will most definitely be dismissed and mocked by those with closed minds but, as we can see by the aforementioned cases, the sceptics have an abysmal track record so far!

This book is about ghosts – whatever they are. Every culture has believed in ghosts at one time or another. The Buddhists tell us that Buddha trained himself to overcome fear by sitting in a haunted cemetery and in the Iliad, the Greek writer, Homer, describes the ghost of Patroclus visiting his friend Achilles at the dead of night, to plead for a quick funeral so that he might be swiftly released from the pain of his earthly ties. Spooky tales are not just a contemporary phenomenon – in fact, there are several ghosts mentioned in the Old Testament.

In the course of a person's lifetime, the chances of encountering a ghost are surprisingly high. The statisticians say that only one person in ten has seen a ghost, but this figure is only based on the body of data acquired from people who have dared to admit that they have had a paranormal encounter.

Society's attitude to the paranormal has always been largely hypocritical. There are many people who mock the supernatural but believe their lucky numbers will come up on the lottery one day, or who check the horoscope column of the daily newspaper to see what the stars have in store!

In the meantime, hardly a month goes by without news of a haunting. Many serious psychical research groups are now combating society's ignorance of the psychic by approaching universities, where they hope the paranormal will one day be recognised as a branch of science. Already, at the University of Edinburgh, a Chair of Parapsychology has been created and in London, the Koestler Foundation is an open-minded institution, dedicated to researching areas beyond the borders of what can be explained by our present science.

In a landmark ruling in July 1991, the New York Supreme Court officially acknowledged the existence of ghosts when it legally opened the way for a husband and wife to sue the former owner of the house they had bought, for the return of their $32,000 deposit. Jeffrey and Patrice Stambovsky were allegedly driven from their luxurious 18 room riverfront house in Nyack, New York, by two spectres which evidently dated from the days of the American Revolution.

The five Appeal Court judges voted three to two to declare that, as a matter of law, the Stambovsky's house was haunted, overturning a ruling by the trial judge. In times to come, the Stambovsky case will no doubt be regarded as an important milestone in the annals of the paranormal.

Many of the stories within this book originated from the numerous letters and phone-calls I received at Radio City, Liverpool's independent radio station, where I present a regular slot about ghosts and local mysteries on the Billy and Wally show. The show is probably the most popular one in the north-west region, and the response from the listening public was tremendous, confirming my suspicions that a large segment of the population is fascinated by the paranormal.

Why do scientists reject the idea of ghosts? Well it seems that most scientists think phantoms run right against the grain of good old commonsense. When a person dies, that is the end of the story and, until someone returns from beyond the grave to take part in a repeatable controlled scientific experiment to prove survival of death, ghosts do not exist.

That is how most scientists view the subject of the paranormal but they have often had to rethink their opinions. For example, in 1803, Thomas Young carried out an experiment that showed, without a shadow of a doubt, that light is a wave of energy. But over a century later, the scientists made a disturbing discovery that light also behaves as if it were a particle. But how can a beam of light be a wave and a particle? It goes right against commonsense. The wave/particle problem is so baffling that even Albert Einstein and Stephen Hawking have failed to crack it. So, if the greatest minds of science are at a loss to explain the nature of light and gravity, how can they possibly dismiss paranormal phenomena?

# Theories of Ghosts

If we accept that ghosts are real, what are they? How can we explain them? The popular belief is that ghosts are earthbound spirits of the dead which continue to haunt the locality. Let us consider this interpretation.

Apparently, the human brain has the capacity to store, organise and retrieve up to 15 trillion (a trillion is one million cubed) items of information, a capability that seems somewhat excessive for the ordinary requirements of life. However, this complex organ was not always thought to contain a person's consciousness and identity.

Aristotle (384 – 322 BC), the ancient Greek philosopher and tutor to Alexander the Great, actually believed the brain was simply a minor organ that cooled the blood. The Greek anatomist, Herophilus (330–260 BC), who was the first to systematically dissect a human body to compare it with the viscera of other animals, knew better than Aristotle and correctly recognised that the brain was the seat of intelligence. But the thinkers of the day could not accept this, opting for Aristotle's theory instead.

Approximately 1,900 years later, Thomas Willis (1621–1673), an English physician, rediscovered the theory that the brain contained the mind after noting that nerves all over the body led into the skull. After taking 1,900 years just to locate the brain, scientists had the daunting task of working out how the brain functioned. They are still not absolutely sure, but the brain seems to be made up of billions of intricate interconnecting nerve cells called neurons, as well as supporting cells (neuroglia). The neurons transmit electrical impulses and release chemical transmitters that act on other neurons as well as muscle (or effector) cells. In layperson's terms, the brain is mostly electrical in its workings and electricity is a form of energy. According to science's immutable First Law of Thermodynamics, energy cannot be created or destroyed. So if the energy in the brain can never be destroyed, where does it go to when a person dies? Does it radiate into space like a radio wave; or does it somehow linger around, like a charge of static electricity. If this post-death electrical field was part of a person's consciousness, what would happen if it were transmitted into the developing mind of an embryo? Could a disembodied mind take over the mind of the foetus? Furthermore, could this hypothetical point explain reincarnation?

Let us not digress from our search for the spirit. Long before the neurologists discovered that the brain and nervous system used electricity to function, the occultists had claimed that each person possessed a secondary body made of energy that is stowed away in the physical body. The mystics maintained that this 'etheric' body contained the ego and consciousness and could leave the physical body under certain conditions, especially when the flesh and blood body was very ill or dying. The occultists called this stowed-away entity the 'astral body', although the esoteric terminology isn't important; the Ancient Egyptians called the astral body the 'Ba' and pictured it in their wall paintings as a bird with a human face. Ancient Indian writings tell of eight siddhis (supernormal powers) that can be acquired through meditation. The sixth siddhi is the ability to fly through the sky by releasing the astral body, and there is an interesting account of astral espionage in an early 19th century book known as the Bhagavata Purana. In this amazing tome, there is a story of a girl named Usha, who flies out of her body during sleep to reconnoitre faraway lands and spy on friends living many miles away.

There are also Biblical references to astral travel. St Paul recounts a man he knew who, "whether in the body or out of the body, God knoweth, was caught up into paradise and heard unspeakable words, which is not lawful for a man to utter". (2 Corinthians 12:3)

For years, the idea of an astral body was deemed to be a laughable absurdity by scientists – until the late 1970s, when a number of eminent embryologists came to the conclusion that developing limbs and organs in a human foetus are shaped by morphogenetic fields. This term means fields that give rise to form, or form-fields. The embryologists had wracked their minds trying to fathom out how a human foetus changes from a fertilized egg into a fully-developed baby after a mere 380 days. They could see that something was supervising the highly specialised development of the various parts of the baby's body – and that supervisor was evidently not just the DNA in the baby; something else was at work.

For example, consider your arms and legs. The DNA in these limbs is identical, but they are shaped differently. Something else besides your DNA was responsible for shaping the different parts of your body and this something is still a mystery. The present theory postulates morphogenetic fields as the invisible supervisor. To exemplify this theory, imagine a piece of paper with iron filings sprinkled on it. As soon as we lift a bar magnet to the underside of the paper, without touching it, we only have to tap the paper and the scattered iron filings on top of the paper will instantly align themselves within the magnetic fields from the bar magnet and form complex shapes. Morphogenetic fields work in the same way, but they seem to be more complex and mysterious than a magnetic field.

Recently, it was discovered that if a small electric current (0.2 micro-amperes) is passed across the stump of a frog's severed limb, most of the lost limb will regenerate and grow back. This is something of a breakthrough, because frogs do not usually regenerate lost limbs, unlike the salamander, which can regrow a leg after 11 weeks. Electric currents have also been employed in a similar way to promote bone-healing in humans. All this research indicates that the human body is criss-crossed with fields of electricity and other, as yet unknown, energies. Is the total sum of these energies the fabled spirit body? Is that the part of us that survives the death of the physical body? If it is, could this explain ghosts?

Sceptics will say at this point that all the things we have mentioned so far are invisible; the astral body, morphogenetic fields – even the spirit. But there are so many invisible things in this world which we take for granted. The invisible electromagnetic waves in our microwave ovens that cook our meals, the television signals that are broadcast to our satellite dishes and television aerials, bringing us news, films and soaps; the FM and AM waves that bring chat and music to our radios; the ultraviolet rays that our sunbeds tan us with and even the digital signals that take our voices down the optic-fibre cables of the telephone network; all these are invisible to us, yet they are real. If we take a look at the whole range of radiations known to man, we can see that our eyes can only perceive a very narrow band of radiation which contains all the colours known to us. All the colours which make up the great works of art, from Da Vinci to Dali, are contained within an extremely slender strip of the electromagnetic spectrum.

Our sense of hearing is also as limited as our vision. The deepest sound we can hear has a wavelength of 22 metres and a frequency of 15 cycles per second. The shrillest sound a human adult can hear has a wavelength of 2.2 centimetres and a frequency of 15 000 cycles per second, although children can hear just above this range. Certain animals can hear shriller sounds that bypass our hearing. Bats emit squeaking sounds with ultrasonic frequencies in the range of 13 000 cycles per second and navigate by listening to the echoes of these sonar-type waves. The hearing range of the domestic dog also extends into the ultrasonic; that is why humans cannot hear the sound of a dog whistle.

So, when we realise that there are radiations and sounds beyond our range of perception, we should be less doubtful about the reality of spirits.

I believe that some ghosts are spirits, while others are nothing more than images from the past that are occasionally replayed like a video-recording. Who, or what, is replaying these images of bygone days is anybody's guess. Some physical researchers think the weather may be a contributing factor; that under certain temperatures, perhaps when the Earth's magnetic field is unusually intense, something happens to the very fabric of the space/time continuum, and phantoms of people long-dead walk through our dimension. Other freethinkers believe that the mind of the person who sees the ghost is responsible. Perhaps these people have abnormalities in the parts of their brain that deals with vision; however this theory does not explain cases where two or more people have simultaneously witnessed an apparition.

Some people have asked me where all this delving into ghosts will lead to. In other words, what's the use of chasing spectres? I always tell them that one day, when ghosts are understood, we may be able to communicate with people we had long thought were dead. Perhaps loved ones, personages of immense historical interest, or great intellectuals, such as Einstein and Plato, could communicate with us once again. Mozart and Beethoven could again bestow soul-stirring symphonies to the world. The possibilities are immense. And should we discover how to induce ghostly holograms from the past through some electronic manipulation of time, the whole panorama of the past would be opened for our inspection. History would no longer be a clutter of surmises and educated guesses, although, of course, reading about battles, plagues, inquisitions and massacres is one thing; but seeing such brutalities re-enacted before us and knowing that we cannot help those victims of violence would be quite another. If psychical research one day reaches a stage where a technical breakthrough allows the past to be inspected, then reflect on the possibility that you, the reader of this book, could at this moment be the unwitting subject of a Primitive Psychology class somewhere in the future.

# Haunted Liverpool

Ghosts have long been reported throughout the city and many familiar landmarks have become synonymous, in the minds of many, with the ghosts and paranormal phenomena, associated with them.

## The Ghost Rider of Aintree

Every spring the crowds gather at Aintree for the most spectacular – and controversial – steeplechase in the world; the Grand National. Over four miles long, the National is the ultimate challenge to both horses and jockeys alike and the euphoria the race provides for the punters, often outweighs the tragic side of the event, namely the death of those horses pushed beyond the limit of their endurance.

Such a place is bound to have its share of ghosts. The most regular phantom of the racecourse is the ghost of Lottery, the winner of the very first Grand National in 1839. The spectral steed has been seen galloping along the course and several witnesses have even seen the shadowy outline of the horse's jockey, Jem Mason, crouched on the phantom's back. Those who have witnessed the eerie action replay, say that the horse and its ghost rider disappear after making a mighty leap of 33 feet over the last jump of the course. Lottery was so outstanding in his day that he was barred from being entered in certain events but, because he never followed up his breathtaking win at Aintree, he ended his days pulling a plough.

## Albert Dock Apparitions

Shortly before the opening of the Docklands Cafe Bar at the Albert Dock in 1992, workmen who had been putting the finishing touches to the building reported hearing unexplained voices chattering around them. One electrician refused to work in the cafe after dark because he, too, had heard an unseen entity speaking.

Naturally the reports went unheeded but, when the Docklands Cafe opened, the staff also heard phantom voices and the doors were seen to swing open of their own accord. The waitresses were unnerved by the eerie chattering at first, but gradually became used to the sounds. It was on 15 March when waitress, Susan James, decided she had had enough of the invisible gasbags and she shouted, "come out, come out, wherever you are!"

On the following morning, in the cafe, a napkin was found draped over the till. On the napkin, in shaky, childish writing was the message, "I come out but you gone". When the waitress read the reply to the previous night's challenge, a chill ran up her spine.

The Albert Dock has other ghosts. One of them is the spectre of an early 19th century gentleman, who patrols the shopping malls and colonnades near the Dock's Tate Gallery in the small hours.

He is thought to be the ghost of James Jones, a night-watchman, who fell into the Salthouse Dock and drowned in 1817 after drinking too much whisky.

## The Rodney Street Spectre

Early one morning in 1970, a middle-aged woman who worked as a kitchen assistant at the YMCA in Mount Pleasant, boarded the number 86 bus near her home in Parliament Street at 6.30. At Leece Street, the woman left the bus and headed for her place of work via Rodney Street. She had been taking this route every work day for over six years and was well accustomed to the spooky aura that hung over the site of the derelict ruins of St Andrew's Presbyterian Church. By now, she considered herself quite immune to the eerie atmosphere of that part of Rodney Street.

As she neared the old church ruins, she suddenly found herself confronted with the solid-looking apparition of a top-hatted man in a cape, who came out of one of the walls that surrounded the church's cemetery. The ghost advanced towards the terrified woman, then hesitated, performed a U-turn and hurried back through the wall. Understandably, the woman took to her heels.

The identity of the ghost, which has been seen by many people over the years, including a policeman, will probably never be known. However, not far from the spot where it emerged from the wall, in the grounds of the cemetery itself, stands a giant, sinister-looking pyramidal tomb of a Scot called McKenzie, who was a wealthy promoter of the early railways and a restless advocate of scientific progress. Perhaps he is restless still …

Incidentally, McKenzie left bizarre instructions in his will concerning his internment and so, inside the pyramid, the eccentric Scotsman's corpse is seated at a card table with a winning hand!

## The Haunted Fire Station

One wintry night in 1991, Liverpool fireman, Keith Taylor, was sleeping soundly in his bunk in the rest-room of West Derby Road Fire Station, when he suddenly awoke and was startled to see a man in old-fashioned clothes staring at him. The stranger looked as if he had just stepped out of a Dickensian novel. He sported a top hat and was dressed in Victorian-looking attire. A few seconds passed, then the top-hatted man vanished, leaving Mr Taylor with an unbelievable tale to tell his colleagues.

He was later surprised and relieved to learn that other firemen had already encountered the station spirit. Tony Jordan and Andrew Matheson, two other firemen who shared the night-shift with Keith Taylor, admitted, rather reluctantly, that they too, had been roused from their sleep by spectral figures who pulled at their sleeping bags. Keith Taylor said of his unnerving encounter with the station spook, "it sounds far-fetched and if it had not happened to me, I would never have believed it".

The ghosts of the rest-room appear to be two men who are sometimes accompanied by a group of children. The firemen noticed that the visitations became more frequent after workers building an extension to the fire station discovered an old water-well.

As a last resort, the firemen contacted Coral Matthews, the treasurer of a local Spiritualist Church, and she assigned a medium to investigate the case. The medium visited the station in an attempt to communicate with the spirit and discovered that the ghost with the top hat was Edward Wilson, who is believed to have once lived on the site of the fire station during Victorian times.

In his conversation with the Victorian during a seance, the medium learned that the ghosts were friendly and were merely showing an interest in the work the firemen do.

The medium said it was a common occurrence for non-malevolent spirits to become interested in people who work for the good of mankind: people such as ambulancemen, policemen and, of course, firemen.

## The Witches of Castle Street

The word 'witch' is taken from the Anglo-Saxon word 'wicca', which means 'the wise ones' – a description of a mysterious cult that dated back to the Stone Age. Members of the Wicca cult, witches and warlocks, were invested with forbidden knowledge of the occult and were able to cast good or malevolent spells. Lancashire held the largest population of witches in the country in Mediaeval times and, in the early 17th century, the county was synonymous with the black arts because of the famous Pendle Witches trials.

Liverpool also had its witches. In 1667, Sir Edward Moore, a Liverpudlian landlord, suspected one of his tenants, the Widow Bridge of Castle Street, of being a witch and when she was arraigned, she confessed to being a sorceress, along with her sister, Margaret Loy. The sisters said they had become witches upon the death of their mother – who had also been a witch – 30 years earlier. Having nothing to leave them, their mother had bequeathed them a talking cat that spied upon enemies and an evil spirit that would rob for them.

Instead of sentencing the witches, they were evicted from their house in Castle Street and exiled from Liverpool. They moved to a run-down cottage on a site near what is now Stockbridge Village.

## The Ghostly Policeman of Scottie Road

In August 1971, several residents of Lawrence Gardens, near Scotland Road, spotted a man dressed in an old-fashioned policeman's uniform strolling down the street. They watched, bemused, as he swung his truncheon and tapped doors and windows with it as he walked his beat. One curious resident followed the odd-looking man up the street to get a better look and noticed he was wearing a haversack with a tin helmet attached to it. As the policeman turned the corner of the road, the resident trotted after him. On turning the corner himself, however, the resident was stunned to discover that the policeman had vanished into thin air!

Later, when some of the older folk living in the Scotland Road area heard of the supernatural episode, many of them recalled that there had been a police constable in the 1930s who tapped on doors and windows with his truncheon, to inform the old and infirm that all was well because he was around and to warn criminals and illegal gamblers of his presence.

At the outbreak of the Second World War, that constable, like every officer of the law, was supplied with a rather inadequate-looking anti-shrapnel helmet, or 'tin-hat' as it was nicknamed. Many old-timers claim that he was killed in an air-raid on the seventh night of the now infamous May Blitz of 1941, minutes after carrying a disabled child to the safety of an air-raid shelter.

People who remembered the constable said that the street near Lawrence Gardens, where the ghost was seen, was part of his beat.

## Help from beyond the Grave

On the wintry evening of 16 December, 1878, Doctor Charles Blunden fell asleep at his desk in his surgery in Myrtle Street, after an exhausting day's work. At 7 o'clock the doctor was awakened by the incessant ringing of the doorbell. He answered the door and saw a little ragged-trousered boy, with a blue scarf, standing on the snow-covered step in his bare feet. The doctor quickly invited the poor child in, but the boy refused and cried out: "Please come with me! Mother's ill!"

The doctor grabbed his coat, hat and medical bag and followed the boy to nearby Arrad Street, where a woman lay prostrate in the snow. The doctor took the woman to hospital, where she was treated for pneumonia. After making a miraculous recovery, the woman thanked the doctor for saving her life, but the doctor merely asserted that it was her son who deserved the praise and asked where the boy was. The woman looked puzzled. She told the doctor that her son had died from a fever two years ago. Doctor Blunden was speechless. The woman then produced the item of her son's clothing which she kept as a memento, a blue scarf – identical to the one worn by the barefooted boy.

## The Haunt of the White Lady

It may surprise some people to learn that ghosts are hardly ever seen in graveyards. They apparently haunt offices, fast-food outlets, shopping malls and just about every place where you find people, but cemeteries are low on the list of places they frequent.

However, there is one chilling exception – Toxteth Park Cemetery, the haunt of the White Lady. No one knows who she is, but the barefooted White Lady has been seen for over 20 years, floating across the cemetery in Smithdown Road as she looks at the gravestones. Some say she is looking for her own grave so she can rest in peace. Occasionally she flits into the path of vehicles on the busy main road and is said to have been the cause of a few fatal crashes over the years.

## Phantoms of the Phil

Liverpool's first Philharmonic Hall, which opened in 1849, was regarded in its day as one of the wonders of the musical world. The German-born pianist and conductor, Charles Halle and Jenny Lind, the 'Swedish Nightingale', were just two of the many famous visitors to the Hall. On the night of 5 July

1933, a fire broke out in the Hall and, by morning, the building was a smouldering mountain of rubble. Liverpool had lost its temple of music. Six years later, the new Philharmonic Hall, erected on the site of the old one, was opened by Sir Hugh Allen, an Oxford music professor.

The new Hall soon became as famous as the old one, attracting such musicians as Jean Sibelius, Sir Malcolm Sargent and Sir Charles Groves to perform under its roof but there are also several lesser-known regulars who also appear at the Philharmonic.

Musicians at the Phil have reported experiencing strange, cold sensations in parts of the building, but the men who have actually encountered the ghosts are the night-watchmen. One night-watchman, Frank, who patrolled the corridors of the Philharmonic for over 30 years until his death in 1985, told me of several spooky happenings.

At about 2.30 one morning, Frank was doing his rounds, when he heard a scraping noise in front of him. Flashing the beam of his torch in the direction of the noise, he saw a chair moving across the floor towards him. As it approached, the chair slowed and stopped in front of him.

On another occasion, Frank was in the Green Room when he heard a distinctive knocking on the door. He opened the door but found no one there. The following night, another watchman reported hearing the same ghostly tap. Other watchmen in the building have reported hearing heavy footsteps on the roof at about 3 o'clock in the morning. Sometimes the nocturnal roof-walker descends a stairway on the top floor of the building, then comes to a halt somewhere near the projection room.

Some think that the footsteps belong to an old female opera singer (some say it is Grace Moore) who visited the Philharmonic Hall regularly until she met her death in a plane crash in the late 1960s.

A further encounter occurred in August 1987, when two night-watchmen spotted the apparition of a young-looking woman up in the balcony. As they watched in disbelief, the woman smiled, waved at them, then vanished before their eyes. Her identity remains a mystery.

## Speke Hall's Mystery Ghost

Speke Hall is a half-timbered house dating back to Shakespeare's time and the manor that the house stands in, is so old that it was recorded in the Domesday Survey of 1086. The original inhabitants were the Norris family but, because of financial problems, they were forced to sell the Hall to the Beauclerks, who lived in the south of England. Sadly, the Beauclerks neglected the Hall and it fell into a dilapidated state. Then, in 1797, Richard Watt purchased the building and restored it. (Watt's successors handed over Speke Hall to the National Trust in 1943)

Throughout the comings and goings of the various families who have resided in the Hall, only one inhabitant has remained in the old house and that is the resident ghost! The phantom that walks Speke Hall is believed to be the ghost of Lady Beauclerk but historians say this is impossible because records clearly show that none of the Beauclerk family ever actually visited the Hall.

The unidentified ghost has been seen by many people around the Tapestry Room and one guest, who stayed overnight, encountered the ghost in her bedroom, where it floated through the wall. When that section of wall was later examined, investigators were amazed to discover a secret passage. The function of this passage, which leads downwards through an outer wall, is unknown, although some believe it was a hiding hole for Catholic priests during the time of Cromwell.

## A Chilling Warning

In September 1775, a widow named Daisy Pickett fell gravely ill with pneumonia. She lived in an old house in Harrington Street with her five sons, who ranged in age from 15 to 21. These lads were an argumentative bunch, forever fighting over the pettiest things. Whenever they started to battle, Mrs Pickett would cry, "I won't tell you again! Stop it!" and begin to scream until her boys ceased fighting.

A week after falling ill, Mrs Pickett died. The five boys laid their mother in a tasteful silk-lined coffin for a three-day wake. After relatives and friends had paid their respects, the five sons gathered at a table near the coffin and drowned their sorrows with wine. The drinking continued until 5 o'clock in the morning when the inevitable happened – a fight broke out because the youngest brother claimed his mother had loved him most. The others disagreed and fists began to fly.

Moments later, a familiar voice shouted, "I won't tell you again! Stop it!"

The brothers immediately stopped fighting and looked at their mother's corpse sitting up in her open coffin. Her eyes were wide open but white and blank. She screamed and her terrified sons ran out of the house. They never argued again!

## The Cannibal Captain

This salty spine-tingler is from a news item in an old 19th century newspaper called *the Liverpool Albion*…

In July 1884, a ship named *Pierrot* capsized in the mid-Atlantic with only four survivors. One of them was the captain, Edward Grace, a Liverpudlian.

For three weeks, the four survivors huddled together in a lifeboat with little food and water.

Grace forced the men to draw lots, with the unlucky one among them to be eaten so the others could survive. Two of the seamen agreed, but 16-year-old Richard Tomlin protested. As the young man slept an hour later, Captain Grace slit his throat. Over the next four days, the three remaining men ate the boy's flesh. To stop the body from smelling, the men took bandages from the first aid box, dipped them in salt water and wrapped them around the corpse. When the men were eventually rescued, they were brought to Portsmouth and charged with murder but the Home Secretary thought they had been through enough and commuted their sentences to six months imprisonment.

When Grace had done his time, he changed his name and came to Liverpool to find work. One foggy night, as he walked along Paradise Street, he saw the bandaged, bloodstained figure of Richard Tomlin approaching, holding his hands out. Grace ran for his life but, wherever he went, the thing in bandages followed him.

In panic, he fled to the police and told them about Tomlin's ghost. Thinking him drunk, they threw him in a cell in Anfield Road Bridewell. The following morning they found Grace dead in the corner of his cell, his eyes wide open with fear and a piece of torn bandage in his hand.

## The City in the Sky

On the afternoon of 27 September 1846, the citizens of Liverpool witnessed an extraordinary spectacle – the shimmering mirage of a city's skyline which appeared in the clouds over Kirkdale and remained in full view for over a quarter of an hour.

Liverpool ground to a halt as people stared at the strange ghostly city in the sky. Some claimed they could see towers and domes in the floating city and a local astronomer, a fellow of the Royal Academy, trained his telescope at the mirage but never divulged what he saw.

The mirage gradually faded away as mysteriously as it had appeared and was never satisfactorily explained. Some think that it was just a case of mass hysteria but there have been other sightings of phantom cities in the skies all over the world and scientists believe they are rare optical illusions, like desert mirages, caused by layers of hot and cold air in the atmosphere acting like a giant lens which magnifies distant images.

## Mystery of the Mass Graves

The strangest story I have investigated, so far, began when I received a call at Radio City from a worker on a building site in Old Swan, who said he had had a ghostly encounter with a hooded monk in black who had brushed past him, then faded before his eyes. The same figure had been seen by a group of youths the previous night.

I visited the site and looked into its history and unearthed a macabre mystery. Through my research I learnt that, 3561 bodies in coffins, stacked 16 deep, were discovered in 1973, on the very same spot where the building site now stood. No one has yet explained the Old Swan mass grave.

The Home Office only recently broke its long silence over the suspicious mass burial, by admitting that they could not find any trace of records of the incident. It was not a plague pit, because the plagues of the 15th century never killed more than a few hundred people in Liverpool. Stranger still, the bodies were neatly grouped according to their age. Sadly, before an archeologist could travel up from the British Museum to investigate, the City Council had the bodies cremated.

A smaller mass grave, of around 200 bodies, was unearthed in the early 1960s in Cobden Street, off Everton Road, near St Fabius' Church. None of these corpses was in a coffin and, strangely, most had perfect teeth, a good indicator they were young when they died.

## The Ghost of Billy Jones

During Easter 1993, Mr Wilkinson left his local pub and returned to his home in Wellington Avenue, Wavertree. However, when he put his key in the front door, he discovered that the door would not open.

Concluding that burglars had got in and locked the door from the inside, he called the police. Two policemen turned up and tried the door without success. One of them announced, "looks like we'll have to do a Sweeny!" and, backing up six feet, he charged at the door. However, before he hit the door, it flew open and he went flying into the hall. The policemen were so sure that someone had opened the door from the inside, that they both checked the house, expecting to encounter burglars – but the house was empty and all windows were found to be locked.

At this point, Mr Wilkinson told them that the culprit must have been Old Jonesy – Billy Jones – the mischievous and harmless ghost of a popular headmaster who had died in the house many years before and the policemen quickly returned to their patrol car and sped off!

## The Man in the Iron Tube

On the morning of Friday 13 July 1945, a group of children playing on a blitzed site on the corner of Fulford Street and Great Homer Street, discovered a sheet-iron tube that was partially opened at one end. Through the opening, one of the children saw a skeleton inside the cylinder. The police were informed and it was taken to the City Morgue, where a record was made of the tube's dimensions – 6 feet, 9 inches long and 18 inches in diameter.

When the tube was cut open with an oxyacetylene torch, it was found to contain the six-foot skeleton of a man in tattered Victorian clothing. The skull rested on a brick, wrapped in sacking. The cadaver wore a morning coat, narrow-striped trousers and a pair of elastic-sided boots. On one finger bone there was a gold signet ring set with a bloodstone and bearing a London hallmark for the year 1859. In the tail pocket of the morning coat were several documents relating to a TC Williams and Company of Leeds Street, Liverpool. Diaries covering June 1884 to July 1885 were also found in the corpse's coat but none of these clues threw any light on the dead man's identity, or why the body was in the cylinder.

In the year 1883, a firm of oil merchants and paint and varnish manufacturers traded under the name of TC Williams and Company at 18-20 Leeds Street, and the principal of the firm was Thomas Cregeen Williams, of 29 Clifton Road, Anfield.

In 1884, the business accounts of this paint firm were being probed by accountants and Thomas Williams was apparently worried about the investigations. It has been suggested that he took refuge in the cylinder to hide from his creditors and probably died from asphyxiation. But why hide in a cylinder? Most debtors in those days simply boarded a ship when bankruptcy loomed. The baffling case remains an enigma to this day.

## Poltergeists and the City Council

Before 1992, Madryn Street, in Toxteth, was only known as the street where Ringo Starr once lived but, in November of that year, the street hit the headlines when a family who lived at number 35 was disturbed by a particularly nasty poltergeist.

This poltergeist announced its presence to the Santos family by levitating the washing machine and bouncing it like a ball across the kitchen. It then picked up the Santos' 13-month-old baby and hurled him across the room. Luckily the baby suffered no injuries. The poltergeist then tried to smother Mr Anthony Santos while he was asleep in bed. The evil spirit continued to wage its war of nerves on the Santos family for three years and, in the end, they begged the Council to move them. In a landmark ruling, Liverpool City Council spent £700 putting the Santos family up in a hotel and Liverpool Housing Trust moved the family out of its haunted home. The 200-year-old house was blessed by a Catholic priest and the dwelling was re-let.

## The Hope Street Body Snatchers

In October 1826, a gruesome event occurred in Liverpool that sent shockwaves of disgust all over the country. It all began when three large casks labelled, Bitter Salts, were loaded onto a ship, the *Latona*, which was berthed at George's Dock Passage, ready to sail for Leith, Scotland.

Hours after the casks were stowed in the *Latona's* hold, they began to give off the unmistakable odour of decomposing flesh and the captain ordered his men to open one of the casks. Inside, they discovered several human bodies squashed together, packed in salt. There were 11 bodies altogether in the three casks.

The police soon traced the man who had carted the casks to the *Latona*. He told how a tall gentleman, dressed in black, with a Scottish accent, had given him two shillings to take the cargo of corpses to the ship from a cellar at 8 Hope Street. When the police arrived at the house, Reverend James McGowan told them he had recently rented the cellar to a Mr Henderson, a Scot from Greenock, who was in the business of exporting fish oil.

The police asked the vicar for the cellar key and when he said he did not have it, the policemen used a crowbar to gain entry, despite the reverend's threat of legal action for unlawful entry.

When the door to the cellar was forced open, the police recoiled in horror, for, scattered about the cellar were 22 corpses of men, women and children. Mass murder was initially suspected but there were no wounds on the bodies. A subsequent examination of the cadavers revealed that all had died of natural causes and been disinterred from a nearby graveyard in Mulberry Street.

Within days, the police brought most of the Hope Street Body Snatchers to justice and each served a 12 month prison sentence after paying a hefty fine. However, the mysterious Mr Henderson, the mastermind behind the plan to sell the bodies for £15 each to the Scottish medical schools, managed to evade capture.

## The English Civil War Ghosts

In the mid 1980s, a man from a group of paintball combat players got lost in a wood just south of Maghull. He had wandered into a field when he suddenly heard the sound of galloping horses behind him. When he turned around, he was confronted by three horsemen approaching at high speed. He recognised that the riders were dressed as Roundheads from the English Civil War and assumed they were just playing war-games like himself. However, when they came galloping towards him, without slowing, he knew something was wrong and fired his paintball gun at one of the horsemen. The paintball went straight through him and the man fled the field. When he looked back, the Roundheads had vanished.

A farmer later told him that the horsemen had been seen regularly over the years and were thought to be the ghosts of a battle that had taken place in the field between the Roundheads and the Royalists in 1648.

## The Old Man and the Powercut

In December 1993, a National Grid engineer allegedly saw the ghost of a wiry-haired old man, with a Don King hair cut, waving to him from the window of a disused power station on the outskirts of Liverpool. A few seconds later, the old man vanished. When the engineer told a colleague about the old man, he replied that he, too, had seen the ghost and that sightings of him were always accompanied by bad luck.

That same week, Merseyside was hit by the biggest power-cut in its history. At 13:13 hours on 13 December, someone pulled a switch in the disused power station where the ghost was seen. This switch turned on the sprinkler system which showered a massive National Grid transformer with water. The transformer short-circuited and all the power to Merseyside was lost, leaving over five million homes, factories and offices were without electricity.

A National Grid spokesman later admitted, "no one can explain how the sprinkler shorted the transformer".

## The Valentine Ghost

This ghost story happened on Valentine's Day evening in 1874. A young couple, William and Rebecca, were standing on the bridge in Sefton Park, when William said, in a choked voice, that their relationship would have to end because he had been pressured into an engagement with a wealthy heiress. Rebecca cried for a while, then said that life would have to go on but that she would always love him, adding, "dead or alive, promise to meet me here twelve months from tonight at this hour". William did not like the idea, but agreed.

A year later on Valentine's Day at 11pm, William turned up at the bridge. He waited for an hour but Rebecca was nowhere to be seen. At exactly midnight, however, Rebecca turned up at the end of the bridge and William ran to embrace her – and passed right through her! When he looked about, Rebecca was gone. He later learned that, at the same hour, Rebecca had died from cholera at her home in Huskisson Street. According to her nurse, her last words were, "dead or alive, I've got to meet him on the bridge".

## The Ghost of Walton Jail

A violent ghost is said to haunt a cell in Walton Jail. In cell G2, an old lag woke up early in the morning, feeling hands around his throat throttling him. Looking up, he saw they belonged to a black shadow that was leaning over his bunk. As the prisoner let out a mighty scream, it vanished. It transpired that his cellmate had also seen the same shadowy figure the week before, but had told no one.

I researched the case and discovered that in the same cell, in 1927, a convict, William Kennedy, had spent his final hours before being hanged for the murder of an Essex policeman. A week after his execution, warders saw Kennedy's ghost in Cell G2 whenever they looked through the spyhole in the door. Since then, many prisoners have asked to be moved from the haunted cell.

## The Solicitors' Ghost

In 1990, a firm of solicitors in Liverpool kept having trouble with their alarm system. Every night, the alarm would go off but the alarm engineer could not find any fault in the system. Shortly afterwards, fax machines in the office started to switch on and off and the secretaries kept getting nuisance calls from a man calling himself Roy. He told one secretary that he used to work in the building where the solicitors were sited and would giggle as he accurately described what the secretary was wearing, even down to the type of underwear she had on. The calls were finally traced to an empty room above the solicitors' office. There was no phone and none had been connected for over 20 years.

The calls stopped, until one afternoon when a secretary was working at her word processor and she felt the temperature suddenly drop. Something brushed past her back and she naturally jumped and looked about, but no one was there. Then, as she stood up, something pinched her bottom! The secretary let out a scream and ran out of the office to her boss, who calmed her down. He accompanied her back to the office and was horrified to see words being typed on the screen of the word processor. The ghost was typing out little intimate details about the boss's extra-marital affairs. The last line read, "Roy knows".

Two psychics who held a seance at the haunted office said they felt the presence of the spirit of a man who had died in the 1930s, named Roy Sykes. Roy had been a clerk – and also something of a sex pest – at an office in the building now occupied by the solicitors.

The ghostly goings-on at the office gradually faded, but the alarm system still malfunctions from time to time for no apparent reason!

## The Mysterious Mr Moore

The son of a man who worked as a porter at a hotel called The Bee Hotel, which stood in Queen's Square, informed me of a strange story his father had often told him. The tale was of a hotel guest, George Moore, who had stayed at the hotel in the 1930s. George Moore had had a sinister knack of foretelling tragedy and could allegedly tell a person how long they would live.

On 26 June 1936, everyone rushed out of the hotel and looked skywards at the Hindenberg – Germany's giant Zeppelin, which was returning from New York, homeward-bound for Hamburg. As the ship passed over the city, one of the guests said he would love to fly in the Zeppelin and Mr Moore remarked, "that ship will go down in flames".

Exactly one year later, the Hindenberg, which was full of inflammable hydrogen gas, exploded in a fireball in the skies of Lakehurst, near Boston, killing 36 people.

When an American guest booked into the hotel before the outbreak of World War II, Moore told him that America should be ashamed for sitting on the fence. The American replied it was Europe's war.

"It won't be when Pearl Harbour gets hit," retorted Moore.

The American had not heard of Pearl Harbour until Japan attacked it, two years later, in 1941.

Moore also predicted the Apollo moon landings and the Channel Tunnel. He also made one prediction that has not yet come about – that the British Monarchy would be ousted by four foreign men of a political party with a circle of stars as its symbol. Sound familiar? He also prophesied that a generation would come that would dance to the beat of a machine and choose pleasure pills in place of alcohol for leisure. Was he referring to members of the techno-rave generation who have largely dispensed with traditional leisure drinking and opted for designer drugs like Ecstasy?

## The Treasure Ghosts

After presenting my Radio City slot about the paranormal, I received a call from a man in Hale, who told me of an encounter he had had with a phantom monk in Hermitage Road. He said five other people had seen the hooded apparition over the period of a fortnight and asked whether I had heard of the spectre.

I admitted that I had not and began to research the history of the haunted site. I was very surprised to learn that, in 1536, treasure was buried near a lane under the estate of Richard Leycester. This lane lies beneath Hermitage Road. The treasure was buried by the Prior of Birkenhead Monastery, who had come across the Mersey to escape henchmen of King Henry VIII (during the dissolution of the monasteries), who wanted the Monastery's substantial funds. No one has ever reported finding the treasure, so get your metal detectors out!

The Bluecoat Chambers in School Lane, which dates back to the early 18th century, is said to be haunted by a ghost, wearing a three-pointed hat, who has been seen looking out of the central window under the clock which stands above the main entrance to the building.

In 1975, the child of an American tourist saw the apparition looking out of the window at him. The child began to make faces at the ghost, and the ghost allegedly made them back! When the child's father asked who the actor in the period clothes was, staff replied that there was no such person on the premises and calmly told the Americans that they had probably just seen the Bluecoat ghost.

Two separate mediums have looked into the case and believe the spectre is the earthbound spirit of a Scotsman who cannot 'move on' because he left behind buried stolen loot, somewhere near School Lane. The mediums also felt the ghost had a Jacobite connection.

## Tuebrook's Invisible Resident

The oldest dwelling place in Liverpool is Tuebrook House in West Derby, a property dating back to 1615.

The stone-floored, oak-beamed residence has a tiny secret room sandwiched between the two chimneys. There is no access to this hideaway, because the entrance was sealed up many years ago. However, something seems to be living in this room, because footsteps and voices have been heard emanating from it.

One legend is that it was the final refuge of a Catholic fugitive, hiding from Cromwell's soldiers, who died from a heart attack as the Roundheads searched the building for him. The grey image of an indefinable person has been seen flitting about Tuebrook House, when an old clock strikes midnight. Sometimes door latches rattle and floorboards pop up to herald the materialisation of the spectre and, occasionally, the sound of a horse galloping up to the front of the building accompanies the supernatural epiphany.

## Ghosts in Little Crosby

Little Crosby, on Liverpool's northern fringe, is a favourite weekend destination for many families. In January 1995, a couple and their son were walking through the grounds of Crosby Hall, when the mother noticed that, suspended from a nearby oak tree, were two lengths of rope with tyres on each end. Although there was no breeze that day, one of the tyres was swinging back and forth as though a child were playing on it. The other tyre was quite still.

A couple of hours later, the family returned and were amazed to see the tyre still swinging to and fro. No one was near the swing to push it, for the family were the only people in the grounds on that cold January day. They stood in disbelief, waiting for the tyre to stop swinging, but it did not, so they went home with a very perplexing tale to tell!

Little Crosby has more ghosts. One of them is a lady in white robes who has been seen mostly at Christmas at St Mary's Church. For some reason, she only appears to people who work at the church. She simply smiles at them and vanishes.

## The Ghost of James St Station

In January 1996, Radio City presenter, Billy Butler, received an interesting letter from James Davidson, a lollipop man, who lives near Penny Lane. Mr Davidson wrote about two very strange encounters he had had at James Street Station in the summer and autumn of 1995.

Mr Davidson had been going to Hoylake at 10 o'clock in the morning on the first occasion. On the train, he noticed a man dressed as a First World War officer in the compartment. Mr Davidson naturally assumed he was either in fancy-dress or was an extra in some period drama being filmed in the area.

The only thing that seemed unearthly about the military man was his flatness – he looked two-dimensional, as if he were a cardboard cut-out. The stern-looking soldier got off the train at James Street Station and marched along the platform towards the out-of-bounds area at the end, where the tunnel leads to the Wirral.

Mr Davidson – and other witnesses – watched the man, carrying a baton, stride towards a brick wall, walk into it and vanish! Mr Davidson and the other eye-witnesses looked on in utter disbelief. "I wasn't scared," he wrote, "just absolutely mesmerised!"

Mr Davidson saw the ghostly officer repeat the eerie scene in front of dumbstruck commuters in autumn, 1995. About this time, the *Liverpool Echo* ran a small piece about the ghost, reporting that commuters had seen a soldier disappearing into a wall on the underground. Research has since established that a colonel died on the railway line at James Street Station around 1919, but it is not known whether it was an accident or a suicide.

Unlike most witnesses who encounter a ghost, Mr Davidson made a sketch of the phantom he had seen. I have interviewed him at length and find him a very sincere and intelligent man. I have also traced two other witnesses who saw the station ghost and their accounts are identical to the description of events made by Mr Davidson.

## The Penny Lane Poltergeist

In 1930, a family living in Penny Lane was startled out of its sleep by loud noises and thudding footsteps coming from number 44, the unoccupied shop next door. The source of the racket was sought, but to no avail and every night the sound of the restless walker prevented them from sleeping. In the end, the tormented neighbours decided to escape the nightly cacophony and another, unsuspecting family, moved in to take their place.

The new neighbours of the Penny Lane ghost had no knowledge of the previous family's predicament and they soon settled down into their new home. Then, one night in 1945, the sounds of a heavy tread and an unearthly voice were heard. The family knew the sounds were coming from the shop next door but could not fathom out what was making all the noise and many more noisy, nerve-shattering nights followed.

After a long hiatus, the poltergeist came out of retirement and, in January 1971, gave an unprecedented performance. At the time, number 44 was a printing shop owned by Ken Shackman and John Hampton. When Ken and John had left the premises, the sounds of someone pacing the floor of the empty shop grew to such intensity, that neighbours complained to the police and to the shop's owners.

The police investigated the matter with the usual scepticism they show when they look into such matters, but drew a blank. However, Ken and John remained open-minded about the ghost and decided to research the history of the house.

After a journalist from the *Liverpool Echo* wrote a number of articles on the ghost's activities, Shackman and Hampton were inundated with letters and phone calls from ex-Penny Lane residents who had heard the noisy spectre.

These included a woman who had lived nearby, when a child, and had encountered a supernatural entity after the First World War.

The woman wrote to say that she had heard the sound of feet walking heavily on stone steps while in her bedroom one night with her four sisters. Shortly afterwards, the figure of a young woman materialised in front of her. The phantom girl just stood there for a few minutes, calmly combing her long locks of blonde hair before vanishing.

Eager to get to the bottom of the mystery once and for all, Ken and John resorted to a thorough search of the printing shop and had the floorboards taken up, walls checked, furniture examined and the roof inspected. When the search failed to throw any light on the matter, they equipped themselves with a tape-recorder and sat up all night in the house next door.

It was to be a night to remember. The tape rolled and the two brave men waited anxiously for the ghost to walk. They did not have to wait for long! After some banging and shuffling, pandemonium broke out and the walls began to vibrate. At the end of the vigil, the amateur ghost-hunters rewound the tape and listened. The tape had actually recorded the sounds of the ghost – conclusive proof that the phenomenon was not of a psychological origin.

Ken and John and their neighbours noticed that the ghost was most active on Friday, Saturday and Monday nights, but why these particular nights is anybody's guess.

In time, the ghostly noises became fainter and fainter until the nights at the printing shop were filled with an uneasy silence. Today, 44 Penny Lane is a pottery shop. The new residents have not reported any nightly disturbances but the Penny Lane Poltergeist might make a comeback yet!

# Haunts of the Drinker

The local pub has always been the focal point of conversation in the neighbourhood. Long before the advent of the karaoke machine and the giant television screen, the public house was a popular place to exchange stories and to voice opinions on everything from sport to religion.

As closing time loomed, around the eleventh hour, talk would often turn to stories about the unexplained – the devil waiting in his black coach outside the pub to take the drunken reprobates to hell; urban myths about hitch-hikers in the area who were escaped serial killers and so-on.

Of all the tales told by these intoxicated storytellers, none made you shiver more than those which involved the very pub you were drinking in. These tales were too close to home, although some of the yarns were probably just frightening tactics, used by the landlord, to get rid of stubborn clientele. There are some pub ghost stories, however, that are hard to explain away, because so many people who have been unaware that the pub is haunted, have witnessed strange things on the premises.

## The Railway Inn

The Railway Inn, in Wellington Road, Wavertree, for example, has two solid-looking ghosts who are often mistaken for a couple of the locals. One is a young man in a white T-shirt, the other is an old man in a green coat. A barmaid, Jennifer, saw the old ghost go into the men's toilet – but it never came out again. When Dennis, the pub landlord went into the toilet there was no one there. The two ghosts are seen quite regularly by the staff and drinkers but no one knows their identity.

## The Coach and Horses

The Coach and Horses in Low Hill, Everton, also has two spectral regulars. One of the ghosts is a dark, amorphous figure that manifests its presence by resting its dismembered hand on the bar. The drinkers who frequent the pub have nicknamed the chilling entity 'George'.

Christine Tierney had only been landlady of the pub for a year when George emerged to perpetrate a cowardly act. Christine was horrified to discover her 18-month-old son lying fast asleep on the floor of his room, only moments after she had put him in his pram.

Mrs Tierney took the child to hospital but doctors could find no bruises on him. He had not fallen out of his pram and had slept right through the supernatural incident. The finger of suspicion pointed firmly at George!

Shortly afterwards, Joe Downs, a regular, came out of the pub's toilet as white as a sheet. Although Joe never divulged what he had seen, he now refuses to go to the toilet alone.

According to people who have seen George, the apparition has been described as looking similar to the Predator creature from the Arnold Schwarzenegger film. It is sometimes transparent, but its outline distorts the background when it moves, like a pane of flawed glass.

George's identity is unknown, but he is thought to be the ghost of a previous landlord of the pub, who hanged himself in the cellar. In 1995, George solidified into the image of a realistic-looking man who helped a female regular to stack chairs when the pub had closed one night.

Landlady Christine said, "when she had finished, she asked me if I was going to offer the man a drink for helping her. I had to tell her that we were the only ones in the pub. There was no one else about. She was quite shaken!"

George's ethereal associate is a tall figure who appears to be wearing a top hat. The ghost's identity is also open to speculation.

## The Philharmonic

The Philharmonic, in Hope Street, is said to have a lucky ghost. It is alleged that drinkers who have seen the shape of an old man in a grey cloth cap and shabby raincoat in the parlour, have had luck in gambling – especially with the Pools, the Lottery and the Grand National.

But beware, a rather disturbing visitation has also been encountered on three occasions near the pub – a banshee. This Celtic entity was first seen in February 1994, when Philip, a student, left the pub with a couple of friends around 11 o'clock at night. As he passed the alleyway at the Hardman Street side of the pub, he heard sobbing. He stopped and noticed the figure of a woman with long white hair, which covered her face, crying in the dark alley.

Philip sensed that there was something other-worldly about her and quickly rejoined his friends. When he arrived at his bedsit in Ullet Road, he received a phone call from his mother in Kent. His father had died from a heart attack at precisely 11 o'clock that night. Philip immediately thought of the woman in the alleyway. Was the woman an Irish banshee who appears to those about to lose a relative or friend?

A worker in a restaurant told me that he and a friend also saw a woman with long white hair not far from the Philharmonic pub. The two men were white-washing a cellar, when the sound of crying above them made them look up. The time was about 2 o'clock in the morning. Standing on a grid above them was an old, white-haired woman in a black dress. They could not see her face because the long white hair covered it. The woman stood there for ages before moving away at 2.50am, The following morning, one of the nightworkers went home to find his mother dead in her armchair. She had suffered a massive stroke. This probably happened at 2.00am, when a neighbour heard her cry out.

## The Lister

The Lister, in Prescot Road, is often visited by two regulars who perished in a car crash years ago. These two gentlemen have been seen sitting in a corner of the pub quaffing phantom pints of their favourite beverages. On one occasion, one of the ghosts gave a wolf whistle to a new barmaid, who was flattered – until she turned around and saw that her admirer and his friend had vanished, along with their ectoplasmic pints!

## The Rose and Crown

A talkative spook once amused locals at The Rose and Crown pub in Derby Road, Huyton, when a singer was testing his microphone. The singer kept reiterating the irritating phrase, "testing, testing, one-two, one-two," over and over, when a voice from nowhere suddenly added, "three!" The invisible comic has also allegedly spoiled quizzes by shouting out the answers in a raspy voice.

## The Castle

A strange ghost of an old woman in a lace mop cap and a black shawl, who laughs and dances while holding a bottle of beer above her head, has been encountered at The Castle, in Tatlock Street, in Everton. When anyone speaks or approaches her, she vanishes.

# The Story of Spring-Heeled Jack

In Victorian times, Barnes Common, an isolated tract of land on the southern bank of the Thames, was a place to avoid. Travellers foolhardy enough to cross the common during twilight hours, were often attacked and robbed.

One evening, in 1837, a businessman, who had been working overtime at his office, decided to risk a short cut across the common on his way home. A figure suddenly vaulted high over the railings of the cemetery – as if propelled from a springboard – and landed with a thud in front of him. The businessman turned and fled when he saw that the mysterious leaper had pointed ears, glowing eyes and a prominent pointed nose.

Three girls encountered the same sinister figure the following night. Again, he made his appearance by bounding over the railings of the cemetery but, on this occasion, he displayed a violent streak. One of the girls had her coat ripped by him, but managed to flee, closely followed by one of her screaming companions. The third girl tried to scream as the unearthly-looking stranger grabbed at her breasts and began tearing off her clothes, before leaving her unconscious.

During the following month, the leaping terror struck again. This time the venue was Cut-Throat Lane, Clapham Common. After visiting her parents in Battersea, Mary Stevens, a servant, headed back to her employer's household on Lavender Hill. As she strolled through the entrance of Cut-Throat Lane, a tall figure, dressed in black, jumped out of the darkness and threw his arms around her, holding her in a vice-like embrace. Before she had a chance to scream, the stranger kissed her face, then dipped his hand into her cleavage, before laughing hysterically. The girl screamed and the stranger released her and ran off into the darkness.

A number of men hurried to the distressed girl and, after calming her down, they listened to her account of the attack. The men immediately searched the neighbourhood for the mysterious assailant, but without success. The following night, the attacker appeared again, not a stone's throw from the house where the servant girl worked.

That night, the demonic figure bounded out of the shadows into the path of an approaching carriage. The horses pulling the carriage bolted in fright and a terrible crash ensued, injuring the coachman. The mayhem-maker then seemed to defy the law of gravity, as he jumped effortlessly over a nine-foot high wall. Not long after that superhuman feat, a mysterious high-jumping man with a cape attacked a woman near Clapham Churchyard.

Gradually, the news of the satanic superman spread and the public gave him a name – Spring-Heeled Jack. In February 1838, 18-year-old Lucy Scales, and her sister Margaret, were on their way home in the evening, after visiting their brother's house in the Limehouse area.

Suddenly, the terrifying cloaked silhouette of Spring-Heeled Jack leapt out of the darkness and exhaled a jet of blue flames, from his mouth, into Lucy's face. The teenager screamed, her legs collapsed under her and she fell to the ground, blinded. Jack jumped high over his victim and her sister, landed on the roof of a house and bounded off into the night.

A pattern was emerging. Jack seemed to like molesting and terrifying young females. His next attack, which took place two days later, was also on an 18-year-old girl, Jane Alsop. Jane's house was in Bearhind Lane, a quiet back street in the district of Bow, where she lived with her father and two sisters. She was spending the evening reading when, just before 9 o'clock, there was a knock on the front door. Jane answered and outside in the shadows stood a caped man. He said to Jane, "I'm a policeman. Bring a light! We've caught Spring Heeled Jack in the lane!" Jane ran excitedly back into the house and returned with a candle. Offering the candle to the caller, she beheld a nightmarish sight. The flickering light illuminated the face of the man purporting to be an officer of the law. It was Jack and he grinned as he studied the girl's shocked expression.

Before she could move, he spurted out a phosphorescent gas, which partially blinded Jane, then started tearing at her clothes. Jane punched his big nose and managed to give him the slip but the enraged Jack bolted after her and stopped her from re-entering the house by clutching her hair. His claw-like hands scraped her face and neck but Jane's screams alerted her sisters, who came running out of the house and they managed to drag her from her attacker. The three sisters retreated indoors, with Spring-Heel in hot pursuit and, in the nick of time, the door was slammed in Jack's face.

When Jane was quizzed by the Lambeth Police Court about the assailant's appearance, she described a very unusual person:

"He wore a large helmet and a tight-fitting costume that felt like oilskin. But the cape was just like the ones worn by policemen. His hands were as cold as ice and like powerful claws. But the most frightening thing about him was his eyes. They shone like balls of fire."

Two days later, Jane's description was strengthened by the testimony of a butcher from Limehouse. He was the brother of Lucy and Margaret Scales – the victims of the Green Dragon Alley attack.

Accounts of Spring-Heeled Jack's cowardly assaults on the ladies of South London soon spread, scaring many into staying indoors after dark, while others decided to organise vigilante patrols.

A week after the attack on Jane Alsop, Jack called at a house in Turner Street, off Commercial Road. A servant boy answered the door, and Jack, shielding half of his face with his cloak as he stood in the shadows, asked the boy if he could talk to the master of the house. The youngster was turning, about to call for the master, when Jack made the mistake of moving out of the shade into the lamplight. The boy recoiled in horror when he saw the caller had bright orange eyes. As he stood there in a state of shock, he noticed two other details about the mysterious caller; he had claws for hands and, under his cloak, an intricate embroidered design that resembled a coat of arms with, below this design, the letter 'W' embroidered in gold. The boy had heard all the spine-chilling rumours of Jack's 'eyes of Hell'. He let out a terrific scream and, within seconds, windows and doors all over the neighbourhood were opening. Jack waved his fist threateningly at the boy, then rocketed over the roofs of Commercial Road.

When the boy regained his senses, he was cross-quizzed and interrogated repeatedly by the authorities about his hair-raising encounter. His inquisitors wondered what the significance of the embroidered 'W' was and some conjectured that it was the initial of the Marquis of Waterford, widely known as a mischievous prankster. The Marquis was also something of an athlete, but his physical capabilities could obviously not be equated with Jack's superhuman stunts. Even the fittest man in earth could not leap 25 feet into the air, as Jack was alleged to have done many times. In 1859, the Marquis met his death after falling from a horse but the reports of the 'Jack' continued to pour into London police stations and newspaper offices. Spring-Heeled Jack was still at large.

He made an appearance in Lincolnshire one evening, where he shattered the rural tranquillity by leaping over thatched cottages wearing a sheepskin. A mob confronted the laughing leaper and blasted him with shotguns at point-blank range but their firepower had no effect. When the buckshot hit Jack, it sounded as if it was hitting a metal bucket.

One night, in January 1879, a man driving his cart across a bridge on the Birmingham and Liverpool Junction Canal on his way home from Woodcote, Shropshire, was startled when a black, hideous creature, with large luminous eyes, leapt out of a tree and landed on the horse's back. The man tried to knock the beast off the horse with his whip but the creature managed to hold onto the frightened animal, which broke into a wild gallop. When the man got the cart back under control, the 'thing' darted high into the air and disappeared into the trees.

By the end of the 19th century, the geographical pattern of sightings of Spring-Heeled Jack indicated that he was moving in a westerly direction across England, towards Lancashire. In September 1904, the blackguard turned up in Liverpool, where he was seen hurtling down from the roof of High Park Street reservoir. Soon afterwards, Jack gave a typical performance when he was seen clinging to the steeple of St Francis Xavier's in Salisbury Street. Before the awe-struck crowds filling the streets below, Jack jumped suicidally from the steeple and landed somewhere behind a row of houses. The mobs stampeded to see where he had landed and a rumour spread that he had killed himself. The Evertonians were subsequently startled when a helmeted, egg-headed figure in white, suddenly ran down the street towards them. As several women in the crowd screamed, Jack lifted his arms and flew over William Henry Street. After that memorable night, Jack made himself scarce for 16 years.

Then late one evening, in 1920, a man dressed in a radiant-white costume, was seen by scores of witnesses in Warrington's Horsemarket Street, jumping back and forth from the pavements to the rooftops. He finally cleared the town's railway station in one mighty leap and was never seen in the north of England again.

In 1948, the last recorded sighting of a sinister leaping figure, took place at Monmouth in South Wales. Locals who saw a strange-looking man leaping over a stream near Watery Lane, surmised that he was the spectre of a man who had drowned in the stream but the few Welsh folk who were unfortunate enough to encounter the leaper at close quarters, swore he was too solid to be a phantom.

Who or what was Spring-Heeled Jack? Many bizarre theories have been advanced to answer the question. Some said he was an insane acrobatic fire-eater, others believed him to be a dressed-up kangaroo, or a mad inventor who had built an anti-gravity device. One theory that does fit the facts is the alien hypothesis. If we suppose that Jack was from another planet, this would explain his alien appearance, behaviour, his jumping ability and his longevity.

The descriptions of Spring-Heeled Jack's fiery gaze seem to indicate that he had retro-reflective eyes, similar to a cat, which would suggest he was ideally suited to a nocturnal environment. His fire-breathing is not easily explained. Perhaps what Jack really breathed into his victims eyes was not real fire (for none of those attacked suffered burns, nor did the 'fire' ever singe a single hair), but a type of phosphor.

Another unanswered riddle is the fate of Jack. If he was a misunderstood alien, marooned in our world, was he finally rescued, or did he die a lonely death here? We will probably never know.

# The City FM Ghost

In the mid 1980s, City FM, the independent radio station based in Stanley Street, broadcast a ghost story every night on its *Night Owl* programme but, one night, a real ghost turned up and haunted the two disc jockeys and a security guard.

It all started in the early hours one Sunday morning. A radio presenter, waiting in the station's reception area, getting ready to go on air, heard the sound of running footsteps coming down the stairs from the second and third floors of the building. The presenter asked the security guard, who was sitting at his desk, who it could be. The security guard thought it was probably the newsman going to the broadcasting booth but, on checking, discovered that the newsman had not left the newsroom on the first floor. Some unaccounted-for person was in the building.

The presenter and the guard decided to pursue the intruder and started to patrol the building. Reaching a corridor that led to the rehearsal studios, they noticed the air was ice-cold. Proceeding along the corridor, they opened the fire-door that led to another passageway. The strange icy-chill was still prevalent. Suddenly, the fire-door burst open with such force that the walls shook. This unnerved the presenter and the security guard and they stood there, totally perplexed.

Deciding, or rather hoping, that the newsman was playing an elaborate hoax, they ran upstairs to the first floor. However, when they reached the newsroom they found he was busy typing, totally ignorant of the strange events that were taking place downstairs. The presenter and the guard returned to the reception area to find the face of a man pressed against the glass of the main entrance door.

"About time you came back!" said the man at the door, "wasting my time and money".

The presenter looked at the security guard, expecting him to explain what the man was talking about but the guard was no wiser. The man explained that he was a taxi-driver who had come to pick up a young lady who had phoned for a cab about 12.30. The presenter thought this strange because there was no lady in the building and he explained this to the driver, who told him that a girl, calling herself Barbara, had phoned for a taxi to collect her from the radio station.

At 2 o'clock the presenter went on the air. At ten-past-three, the studio lights suddenly went out and he noticed a blonde female whom he later described as being about 21 years of age and dressed very prettily, waving and smiling at him through the studio's glass partition. As he watched, the apparition vanished.

The presenter told a colleague who presented the *Down Town* programme about the phantom but his fellow DJ did not believe him. Ironically, it was this doubting DJ who became the second person to witness the Radio City ghost the next night, as he was presenting *The Peaceful Hour*, a programme which went out just after midnight. At about 12.03am, the blonde spectre materialised and stared at him through the studio's glass partition. The DJ froze, remaining dumb for almost a full hour, until another presenter arrived at the studio. Only then did the terror-stricken DJ break his silence, as he told his fellow presenter of the ghostly visitor.

The station's journalists realised that they had a scoop and called in a group of Preston-based psychical investigators, or ghostbusters, as the media calls them nowadays. The investigators studied the case, looked into the local history of the ground that the radio station stood on and discovered that a flour mill had once stood on the same site as the Radio City building and that Barbara, a young millworker, had lost her life after falling from the fourth floor of the mill.

Numerous presenters continue to claim that the ghost still walks the station's corridors and, occasionally, pays visits to the studios.

# The *President* Disappears

On 11 March 1841, the Atlantic steamship, *President*, sailed from New York for Liverpool. She was a prestigious ship, one of the biggest and most reliable vessels of her day. Her powerful engines, constructed by Fawcett-Preston of Liverpool, had 81 inch cylinders, with a seven and a half foot stroke and were considered a novel design.

Consequently, as the steamer cut through the Atlantic, none of the passengers or crew of the *President* felt anxious about the crossing, on such a state-of-the-art vessel. One of the passengers was Tyrone Power (grandfather of his Hollywood namesake), an actor famous on both sides of the Atlantic. Power had just completed a successful tour of the US and was returning to England.

In the early hours of 13 March, there was a heavy succession of knocks on the door of a house in Blackheath, London, the home of a theatre manager, Benjamin Webster. Mr Webster's butler went to the door and asked who was calling at such an unearthly hour. A voice replied, "Mr Webster! Mr Webster! I'm drowned in the rain!"

The butler thought he recognised the voice as belonging to Tyrone Power, a friend of Mr Webster, but was not sure if he should let the caller in, so he went up to his master's bedroom to rouse him. Mr Webster woke up and, in an irritated voice asked, "what's the matter?"

"Someone is knocking at the hall door. He is calling for you, sir."

"Who's knocking? Don't you know who it is?"

"It sounds like Mr Power's voice, sir. He keeps asking for you. He says he's drowned in the rain," answered the butler.

James Webster got out of bed, put on a heavy coat and ran downstairs, followed closely by his butler. The bolts of the front door were drawn back and the butler nervously rattled the key into the lock and turned it. Old Mr Webster pulled the door open and stared out into the heavy rain and darkness, expecting to see Mr Power, but there was nobody there. Webster closed the door and quizzed his butler over the incident. The butler ran through the details about the mysterious visitor again. Webster felt uneasy because he knew that Tyrone Power had boarded the *President* on 11 March and could not possibly be in England and he returned to his bedroom with a worried look on his face.

By 31 March, the *President* and another ship, the *Britannia*, were overdue and an article appeared in *The Times* highlighting the fact. James Webster read the article and hoped the *President* had not met with disaster. Another week elapsed and still there was no sign of the overdue ships. Relatives of the crew and passengers started to worry. There was a reassuring rumour that the steamship, the *Orpheus*, which had left New York after the *President*, had caught up with her and was accompanying her back to New York because she had had a mechanical breakdown.

However, on 2 April, the *Orpheus* steamed into Liverpool and her captain said he had not set eyes on the *President* once during his journey. Hours after the arrival of the *Orpheus*, the *Virginia* sailed into Liverpool from New York, and her captain, when asked if he had sighted the overdue *President*, gloomily mentioned that there was plenty of ice on the transatlantic route.

On the day after the *Orpheus* and the *Virginia* had docked at Liverpool, the missing steamer *Britannia* arrived in the Mersey. Her captain explained that his ship had suffered damage due to storms, hence the delay, but when he was quizzed about the whereabouts of the *President*, he stated that he had not seen her during his journey, and assumed that she had already docked at Liverpool.

On 7 April, *The Times* published a list of the *President*'s passengers. There were 121 people on board the missing steamship, including the son of the Duke of Richmond, Lord Fitzroy Lennox, as well as the famous thespian, Tyrone Power. The same day, *The Liverpool Albion* printed the following article:

"Nothing whatever has been heard of the *President* steamer. If she had run to southwards and made for the Western Isles for the purpose of replenishing her coal, she is not yet overdue. The Liverpool steamer ( *President*) was, in the winter of 1839, compelled to run to the same islands to replenish her coal, and took 27 days on the passage from New York to Liverpool. Prevalent opinion is that she must have run to the Western Isles and that she may be expected to arrive in a few days. Indeed, there was yesterday a rumour afloat, that the *Lynx* had seen a steamer making for Fayal."

The article seemed to make sense, the *President* could have burnt too much fuel fighting the Atlantic storms, as she had done once before. A report reached London that a special night train had just pulled into a station in Birmingham from Liverpool. A messenger on the train declared that the *President* had docked at Liverpool in a severely weather-battered state but when the authorities in London made enquiries in Birmingham and Liverpool, they learned the story was a cruel hoax and the *President* was still missing. Relatives of the people on the missing steamer broke down and sobbed when they realised that some cruel joker had built up their hopes and dashed them.

When the *President* was three weeks overdue, several Irish ships coming into Liverpool brought some interesting news with them. The crews of these ships swore they had seen a large steamer standing off, waiting for water in the Victoria Channel but, because of the morning haze, none of the witnesses was able to clearly identify the mystery steamship.

The accounts given by the Irish sailors spread throughout Liverpool docks and, that morning, the flag of the consignee was hastily hoisted at the signal station. Lloyd's of London was informed and messages were promptly sent to Tyrone Power's wife and the Duke of Richmond. The news reached the ears of Queen Victoria and, the following day, *The Times* reported that the Queen had expressed the highest satisfaction at the gratifying communication.

Sadly, the Irishmen had been mistaken. The steamer they had sighted was the steamship *Falmouth*, not the *President*. Around this time, a Cork newspaper reported that a bottle had been picked out of the sea which contained a scrap of paper. Written upon this paper were the words, "the *President* is sinking. God help us all. Tyrone Power".

Many dismissed the newspaper report as another hoax. The last rumour about the missing ship came from a Portuguese ship. The captain said he had passed a large steamer that fitted the description of the *President* on 24 May. The unidentified steamer seemed disabled and was drifting in the Atlantic with no sign of life.

Some relatives of the passengers on the missing ship never gave up hope, while others, who had spouses among the missing, remarried and rebuilt their lives. The seafaring communities on both sides of the Atlantic were completely baffled by the steamship's disappearance. If the *President* had gone down in the storms of the 12 and 13 March, why had the vessels following the steamship encountered no floating wreckage? After all, the *President* was a wooden ship.

The *President*'s fate remains one of those unsolved maritime mysteries.

# Admiral Karpfanger

For over a fortnight in 1937, the magnificent four-masted sailing ship, *L'Avenir*, lay neglected in the Liverpool docks. The Finnish-owned vessel had been built in the late 19th century in the era of sail and had been used mainly for shipping grain to ports all over the world. Now, in 1937, such sailing ships were deemed obsolete and the owners, the Erikson Company, had no option but to try and sell the antiquated barque.

The Hamburg-Amerika line was in need of a ship to train its officers and, when its directors heard that the Finnish ship was for sale, they sent the head of their nautical department and a senior engineer from German Lloyd, to Liverpool, to inspect *L'Avenir*.

The two men were pleased at the large barque's condition and immediately started negotiations to buy the ship. Within a few weeks, *L'Avenir* was being towed from Liverpool to Hamburg to undergo extensive refitting. The ship was duly equipped with the latest engines, sonar and a modern radio transceiver. On the outside, *L'Avenir* retained the appearance of an old-fashioned barque but the ship's interior was thoroughly modern.

On 16 September 1937, *L'Avenir*, now re-christened *Admiral Karpfanger*, left Hamburg under the power of her diesel engines with her new master, Captain Walker, an experienced mariner. On board, were 59 people – five officers, a navigation instructor, the ship's doctor, a crew of nine, a carpenter, a bosun, a sail maker and 40 cadets.

Back in their homeland, Hitler was making preparations for his assault on Germany's neighbours but as the *Admiral Karpfanger* cut through the waters of the chilly Atlantic and headed for the southern hemisphere, none of those on board the ship gave any thought to the rise of the Austrian madman. To his closest friends, Captain Walker expressed his feeling that he belonged to the sea because, at sea, he was neither a National Socialist, nor even a German, but a mariner of the world and he cherished this freedom.

On 5 January 1938, the *Admiral Karpfanger* dropped anchor at Port Germein, South Australia, where the vessel took on 42,000 bags of grain. The cadets watched with admiration, as professional stevedores efficiently packed the hold of the ship with the bags and erected wooden bulkheads to prevent the cargo from shifting during the voyage. The journey home to Hamburg commenced on 8 February and Captain Walker estimated they would reach their home port in May, returning via the traditional windjammer route around Cape Horn.

Three days into the journey, a German coastal radio station received a weak short-wave transmission from the ship. The signal was badly garbled and completely unintelligible. Ten days later, Captain Walker tried to radio his position once again but this time the signal was unsuccessful because of atmospheric disturbance. The third message came through clearly and Walker reported that the ship's position was latitude 51 degrees south, longitude 172 degrees east and that all was well on board.

On the morning of 12 March, the German radio station at Nordreich transmitted a message to the second officer on the *Admiral Karpfanger,* informing him that his wife had given birth and congratulating him on becoming a father. At six that morning, the elated second officer replied by short-wave to the radio operator at Nordreich, to thank him for breaking the wonderful news. Captain Walker then radioed a message that he would make his next transmission on 16 March and signed off.

On 16 March, no message from came through. The radio operator listened to the atmospheric howling and static for hours on end but he never heard from the *Admiral Karpfange*r again. The Hamburg-Amerika line issued a statement to the German press to say that the ship's radio had probably broken down but the radio operators at Nordreich continued to listen for a message. April went by and still no message came through and none of the vessels that had passed the barque's estimated position had sighted her, although the Hamburg-Amerika line still insisted the ship was only silent because of a radio fault.

The month of May came and the *Admiral Karpfanger* was expected to enter the Bay of Biscay but the ship was nowhere to be seen. As a training ship, the barque should have made a faster passage than a cargo ship and so, when May passed without a sight of the overdue ship, the ship's owners and relatives of the crew and 40 cadets became very concerned. By 29 June, the missing barque's reinsurance rate was rising steadily on a daily basis. The shipping line instructed the cargo ship, *Leuna,* which was loading in Australia, to make a return journey along the same route as the *Admiral Karpfanger*. Hamburg-Amerika also requested that the Argentine government use its survey ship, *Bahia Blanca,* to look out for wreckage from the missing training ship. The captain of the *Bahia Blanca* did spot the floating vestiges of a ship but it was not from the *Admiral Karpfanger*. The *Leuna* came into Hamburg with no news of the missing ship's whereabouts. The Hamburg-Amerika line sent out other ships to look for it but they all returned without any trace of a sighting.

By 23 August 1938, the training ship was declared as uninsurable on the London market and, by September, the Hamburg-Amerika shipping line had to discontinue its searches for the missing ship and announce that the *Admiral Karpfanger* was officially lost at sea. In response to the announcement, all German ships flew their flags at half-mast. It was a tragedy that cut across the boundaries of nationalism and newspapers and radio bulletins across the globe mourned the loss of so many young lives. The *Admiral Karpfanger*'s fate is still a complete mystery. It seems unlikely that a captain of Walker's experience would have put his vessel on the rocks of Cape Horn.

One report which may throw light on the mystery was largely overlooked at the time. It came from a Captain Pilcher of the British motorship, *Durham*, which had taken the same route as the missing German ship. Pilcher said he had sighted many icebergs – some 500 feet in height and a mile long – on the 24 and 25 of March. Pilcher added that he had never seen so much ice so far north.

In the light of this report, it seem likely that the German training ship hit one of these gargantuan icebergs. If that was the case, why was no wreckage ever found? Yet another mystery from the locker of Davy Jones.

# What *did* Happen to Victor?

We have all heard of mysterious disappearances, like the man who went for a packet of cigarettes and was never seen again, or the little schoolgirl who went for sweets and disappeared off the face of the earth. Some are probably urban legends but the following tale is factual and still a complete mystery.

One cold, autumn night in 1920, Victor Grayson, a Socialist MP, boarded a train at Lime Street Station. Grayson relaxed into his seat and the train steamed off into the night, bound for Hull, where the MP was due to deliver one of his renowned firebrand speeches. What happened next has been the subject of much debate.

When the train from Liverpool arrived at Hull, Grayson was not on board. The police naturally suspected foul play. There were many right-wing extremists who feared Grayson was sowing the seeds of the long-dreaded British Revolution and, without a doubt, there were many in the higher echelons of the glittering champagne society of the 1920s, who would have slept easier with Grayson out of the way.

A massive search was launched covering the six counties between Liverpool and Hull but, after eight weeks, the embarrassed police admitted they could find no trace of the missing MP and called it a day.

Albert Victor Grayson, the son of a carpenter, was born in Kirkdale, a notorious Liverpool slum area, in 1881. There were strange rumours connected with the future political fire-brand's birth and tales of a mysterious, distinguished gentleman, who regularly visited Grayson's mother at her crumbling house in Talieson Street.

The visitor generated a wave of gossip in the neighbourhood and much was made of the fact that someone was evidently financing young Victor's education. Victor did not have a Liverpudlian accent and he later revealed that this was because of the elocution lessons he had received in his younger days.

At the age of 25, he became Member of Parliament for Colne Valley, Yorkshire, but lost his seat in 1910, which was followed by a downward spiral into alcoholism. Upon the outbreak of World War I, Grayson abandoned his pacifism and while he was accompanying his actress wife on a tour of New Zealand, he decided to sign up with the New Zealand Army. He fought at Passchendale with them and was wounded and decorated.

Shortly after the police had abandoned their search for Grayson, there was a sinister twist in the case. Grayson's bag turned up at a London hotel. Police quizzed the hotel manager and he told them that the man who had left the bag had had his head swathed in bandages and appeared to have a badly injured arm. He had left the building with two smartly-dressed men. A painstaking search was made of the room that the mystery man had booked, but it appeared to have never been occupied.

Grayson's relatives and colleagues waited for news of his whereabouts to come in with ever-fading optimism. Some were still of the opinion that the MP had been murdered on the Hull-bound train and thrown from the carriage during the night journey, while others speculated that Grayson had, from the account given by the London hotelier, sustained head-injuries from some type of accident and had probably lost his memory as a result.

The possibility that the man in the London Hotel with the bandaged head may have been Grayson recovering from plastic surgery, was never considered. Why, after all, would the absent MP go to such lengths to disguise himself? As the years passed, it became clear that Victor Grayson was not going to reappear. Rumours spread that Grayson had gone into hiding after being involved in the honours-for-sale scandal of the Lloyd George era but a strange claim that Grayson was the half-brother of Winston Churchill was quickly silenced in a most sinister way. No one knows who started the Churchill rumour but the smear seemed to originate in the House of Commons. It was true that Grayson bore a strong facial resemblance to Churchill but the theory still did not explain the socialist's disappearance.

Then came news of unverified sightings, the most intriguing of which took place in London in 1932, on the top deck of a bus! GA Murray, an old colleague of Grayson, said he was idly looking out of the window near Oxford Street, when he caught a glimpse of Grayson gazing in a shop window. Murray almost fell down the stairs of the bus to chase after his old friend but, by the time the argumentative driver stopped the vehicle, the elusive MP was nowhere to be seen.

Shortly after that sighting, another old acquaintance of Grayson claimed he had glimpsed the evasive MP travelling on the London Underground. A grey-haired Grayson was with an attractive woman who called him Vic and, when the couple left the train near the House of Commons, Grayson nodded towards Parliament and, with a smile, joked, "here's the old firm". Grayson and the woman then disappeared into the milling crowds before the MP's elderly friend could confront him.

When Grayson's mother died at her Liverpool home in 1929, curious crowds flocked to the funeral, expecting the missing MP to put in an appearance, but they were disappointed.

The debonair, well-spoken Grayson, born into poverty, but shielded from destitution by an unidentified benefactor, was soon forgotten, as another fire-brand rose from poverty in Austria to grab the headlines. In 1939, the year Hitler plunged the world into its second world war, an unidentified individual came forward to claim Victor Grayson's 1914-18 war medals. All that is known about this person is that he or she was not from the Grayson family, which adds yet another facet to this unsolved mystery.

# A Maritime Horror Story

Since receiving its first shipbuilding order in 1828, Cammell Laird of Birkenhead has turned out many history-making military vessels such as the American Confederate steamer, *Alabama, HMS Ark Royal* and *HMS Prince of Wales*, the ship that contributed to the destruction of the *Bismark*.

One of the lesser-known vessels from its famous slipway, was the Victorian troopship, *Birkenhead,* the first iron warship to be built for the British Navy. This 1400 ton ship carried the maximum armament and *The Times* called her, "the fastest, most comfortable vessel in her Majesty's Service, and one that can be relied on in hull and machinery".

On 7 January 1852, after several trooping voyages, the *Birkenhead* steamed her way to the naval base at Simonstown, a few miles east of Cape Town, South Africa, en-route for Port Elizabeth. She carried a detachment of the 74th Highlanders, which comprised of 487 officers and men. These troops were urgently needed to reinforce the British Army units in the war with the Kaffirs and many of the soldiers had chosen to bring along their wives and children with them.

For the first ten days of the voyage, the passengers had to endure gale-force winds and unusually heavy seas and many succumbed to sea-sickness, but none aboard the *Birkenhead* could have suspected that much worse was to come. After 47 days, the ship reached Simonstown, where there was something of a crisis. The captain of the *Birkenhead* was ordered by the military to take on coal and horses for the troops and to proceed, without delay, to another port along the coast. Because of the lack of room, the horses were herded onto the *Birkenhead's* main deck.

From Simonstown, the troopship steamed for 500 miles around the Cape of Good Hope towards Algoa Bay, near Port Elizabeth. In the early hours of 26 February, disaster struck. The officer of the watch suddenly recognised a cluster of short lights in the distance and quickly realised that the *Birkenhead* was 80 miles off-course. At 2 o'clock in the morning, the troopship hit a rock, and the force of the impact sent the lookouts reeling across the deck.

A dreadful cacophony of screams filled the night air and the terror-stricken horses on the deck whinnied and stampeded in blind panic. The captain, who had been sleeping soundly in his bunk, was now on deck, still wearing his dressing-gown. He immediately gave orders for the ship's engines to be stopped and instructed his crew to cut the hysterical horses loose. As soon as they were free, the frightened animals galloped across the deck, cleared the ship's rail and plunged into the sea. The horses swam for the shore, but the surrounding waters were heavily infested with sharks and only a few escaped being devoured.

Meanwhile, the *Birkenhead* started to tilt over to starboard and began to sink. Panic gripped the men, women and children but, incredibly, Major Alexander Seton, who was in command of the troops on the ship, managed to get his soldiers under control and soon had them standing to attention, while the civilians were running around like headless chickens, most of them realising with horror, that there were not enough lifeboats on the overcrowded ship to convey everyone to safety.

The captain attempted to back his ship off but this action only damaged further the badly ripped hull and caused the engine room to flood. Women and children were put in lifeboats and lowered into the wintry waters. Fifteen minutes later, as the *Birkenhead* slowly sank beneath the waves, the soldiers went bravely to the end, standing to attention in drill formation. Shortly afterwards, the circling sharks closed in on them.

The wives and the children in the lifeboats, watched in horror as the sharks tore into the soldiers and dragged them screaming under the waves. It is said that, even today, the sharks still congregate in the area where the carnage took place – as if they somehow know about the feast of human flesh that took place there and are still patrolling the waters in the hope that such a banquet may take place again.

How the troopship came to strike Birkenhead Rock (as it is now called) is still a mystery. Some thought that the *Birkenhead's* compass was faulty because of the ship's iron hull, others blame her captain. Whatever the cause, the tragedy is remembered for the amazing courage and discipline of the soldiers who sacrificed their lives for others.

# The *SS Ellan Vanin* Mystery

The sea is a cruel, mysterious mistress, who keeps her secrets well. Her changeable nature can fool the oldest sea-dog – calm one moment, stormy the next. She has spared the lone mariner and sentenced ocean liners and their passengers to an eternity within her dark, uncharted abyss.

For many years, the sea was hospitable to the *SS Ellan Vanin*, a 375 ton Isle of Man steamer that sailed regularly from Ramsey to Liverpool, Scotland and Whitehaven. From 1883, the Manx vessel was a common sight steaming through the Irish Sea and the ship's master, Captain John Teare, had the reputation of a dare-devil because he was never one to be deterred by stormy weather. While other ships were taking shelter from a storm in Ramsey Bay, the *Ellan Vanin* would often be seen steaming for Whitehaven and would return in the evening to be hailed for her bravery by the whistles of the other ships in the bay.

However, one morning, the sea ended its love affair with the little steamer. On 3 December 1909, the *Ellan Vanin* left Ramsey, bound for Liverpool with 14 passengers, a crew of 21, 60 tons of cargo, 88 sheep and several mailbags. The vessel also carried the usual precautionary lifeboats and lifebelts.

As the steamer left Ramsey Bay, there was a moderate north-westerly breeze blowing across the Irish Sea, which promised a speedy crossing. By 6 o'clock, the breeze had become a raging force-twelve gale and huge waves tossed the steamer about like a toy ship as it reached the entrance of the Mersey. It was the worst storm in living memory. Half an hour later, anxious lookouts on the Bar Lightship, watched the distant lights of the inward-bound ship, wondering if the ship would make it to the sanctuary of the Mersey.

Suddenly there was a flash of light from the storm-stricken steamer and all her lights went out simultaneously. The lookouts on the Lightship looked on in horror, for they knew that *Ellan Vanin* had gone under the black icy-cold waves, taking all 35 souls on board with her.

The fate of the steamer seemed so swift to the observers on the Lightship that it almost seemed as if something had sucked the ship under within a matter of seconds.

Five hours later, the Mersey Docks and Harbour Board was informed that the Q1 buoy, anchored at the mouth of the Mersey, had been seen drifting up the river. The Dock Board's vessel, *Vigilant*, which tended the Q1 marker, was sent out to trace the rogue buoy, but the ship found more than a damaged buoy – she encountered the masts of the sunken *Ellan Vanin*, lying broadside to the tide over 1000 yards from the buoy.

Thirty-five feet of the steamer's forepart had broken off. Dozens of lifebelts, the carcasses of drowned sheep and a solitary mailbag had already been found, hours earlier, off Rock Lighthouse at New Brighton and other parts of the wreck turned up at Blundellsands. The *Ellan Vanin*'s saloon clock was washed up on Crosby shore. It had stopped at 6.50am.

It was initially thought that the *Ellan Vanin* had collided with the Q1 buoy but, when investigators from a salvage vessel dived on the wreck, they found a gaping 14 foot hole in *Ellan Vanin*'s port side. What caused this hole in the vessel has never been determined.

Over the following months, several bodies were cast up on the coast, among them a young Manxman who had been on his way to Liverpool to board a ship to New York, where his late uncle had left him a fortune.

Captain William Carter of the salvage vessel, *Salvor*, was puzzled at the state he found the *Ellan Vanin* in after the tragedy. All the passengers' doors had been locked and, although the ship's lifeboat davits had evidently been prepared for turning out, there had been no distress flares fired, which indicated that she must have gone under the waves quite quickly. So quickly that there had not been time for the ship's passengers to put on lifebelts, a puzzle that has never been satisfactorily solved.

# The Ghosts of the Road

The lone night driver knows only too well how roads seem so deceptive and different during the hours of darkness. The motorist's mind at night seems more susceptible to fatigue and our worst enemy in the night – imagination.

Some combat their fear by turning on the car radio, or whistling a tune, others think of mundane matters to stop their thoughts turning to the passing landscape of the night outside – the silhouette of a sinister-looking hitch-hiker, the shadow of a gnarled oak that resembles the outline of the devil. All effects of the mind are enhanced by the way light from sodium lamps plays its subtle tricks on the psyche of the solitary motorist. But sometimes it is not all down to imagination, there are many ghosts reputed to haunt our highways.

One evening in August 1970, a man was driving along Poulton Road from Higher Bebington, Birkenhead, when he noticed a girl with long hair, standing on the verge, further up the road. The motorist stopped by her, wound down the passenger window and asked if she wanted a lift. The girl did not react, so the man opened the passenger door and was astounded to see her slowly vanish in front of him. Many more unwary motorists have offered the ghost a lift before speeding away after witnessing her slow dematerialisation. Some think the roadside phantom is that of a novice from a nearby nunnery, who died in mysterious circumstances after leaving Poulton Hall. At the time of her death, the girl was emotionally torn up over a broken romance.

On the other side of the Mersey, Liverpool's Dock Road has two phantom jaywalkers; a man in a woollen hat, who runs out in front of buses on Sefton Street and a careless individual in a brown overcoat. In February 1996, Avril, from Cheshire, wrote to me about a heart-stopping encounter she had had with the latter.

"About four years ago, I was driving from Runcorn to Crosby via the Dock Road. I drove past the Liver Buildings and then onto the Dock Road and just got level with a gateway to the docks when a man suddenly ran out in front of my car. I know what I saw and it wasn't my imagination. The man was dressed in an old brown overcoat and wore a cap. He looked very antiquated and out of place. I would like to know who this man is and if anyone else has had this experience. The gates are the first gates past the Liver Buildings going towards Crosby."

Another phantom jaywalker seems intent on causing motorists to crash by flitting out in front of them in Higher Lane, Fazakerley. In the past seven years, this dangerous ghost – thought to be a pedestrian who was knocked down in the 1950s – waits at the curb near Sparrow Hall playing fields, then leaps out into the path of on-coming vehicles.

A taxi-driver swerved to miss the spiteful spectre one October night in 1995 and almost crashed into a wall. When he glanced in his rear-view mirror, the cabby saw the shadowy outline of the ghost peeping around a wall, 50 feet away, as if it was surveying the aftermath of the near-fatal accident it had caused.

If you are travelling along the M62, beware of the phantom hitch-hiker who thumbs a lift in the small hours in the Oak Vale Park area. A long-distance lorry driver bound for Northampton from a Liverpool warehouse, made the mistake of stopping for the M62 hitch-hiker in February 1996. Snowflakes the size of goose feathers were falling and Tony, the driver of the HGV, took pity on the middle-aged man standing at the roadside in Edge Lane Drive, wearing an inadequate blue cotton zip-up jacket.

The man hopped into Tony's cab and said nothing.

"Where are you headed?" Tony asked.

"Out of this city," the hitch-hiker mumbled in a low voice.

He then stared through the snow-flecked windscreen at the road ahead, saying nothing. Tony thought the man was odd but harmless and he drove on through the wintry outer limits of Liverpool.

About half an hour later, the silent passenger suddenly said, "there was a terrible crash here. Two people pressed to pulp in an Orion. Flat as a fluke, both of them. A lorry from Ellesmere Port fell on them. Squashed them flat".

Tony shuddered at the grisly account. It got worse. The passenger recounted another gruesome motorway accident ten minutes later.

"Two joyriders crashed at this junction up here. One died, but his body was in the way of the survivor, so the emergency services had to cut through his body to get to the other lad. It was the only way they could get to him. The survivor was conscious through it. Must be a nightmare seeing your best mate being cut in half with a rotary saw."

By this time, Tony was passing Knutsford on the M6. He felt nauseous with the hitch-hiker's macabre blow-by-blow accounts of all the pile-ups that had taken place on the motorways over the years. He pulled his vehicle to a halt on the hard shoulder and ordered the morbid passenger out. The passenger did not flinch, so Tony bellowed, "get out!" and, this time, the gloomy hitch-hiker got out without saying anything.

Tony drove off, relieved, and turned on the radio for company. Shortly afterwards, near Stoke-on-Trent, he was astonished to see the same hitch-hiker standing at the side of the road. How on earth could he have travelled from Knutsford to Stoke in such a short time, he wondered. Glancing in his rear-view mirror, he again was amazed to see the hitch-hiker jumping up and down in a rage, shaking his fist. Thirty miles on down the motorway, Tony saw the same man standing by the roadside, which was a real mystery, as no traffic had passed the lorry driver.

When Tony told his colleagues, they calmly told him that he had merely encountered the M62 ghost, that was all. Tony felt faint when he realised he had invited a ghostly hitch-hiker into his cab.

# Ghosts on Film

It is a sad fact of life that in most cities nowadays, closed-circuit television cameras are watching us like unblinking hawks as we walk down the street. Someone who contacted me at Radio City, in January 1996, informed me that people are not the only things the omnipresent CCTV cameras are videoing. According to a mole who worked in the secretive public and traffic surveillance headquarters in Liverpool, the police possess several videotapes of phantoms that have been captured on camera strolling along the streets. One tape allegedly shows a shimmering phantom crossing Hope Street, walking through the bonnet of a taxi driven by a terrified cabby. The ghost is seen walking up Myrtle Street and turning into Sugnall Street.

There are also phantom vehicles that haunt our roads. A phantom coach from Victorian times has been seen for over 30 years silently rushing past the Muncaster pub in Irlam Road, Bootle. In 1992, a drinker on his way home suffered a minor stoke after stepping into the path of the ghostly carriage. Upon regaining his power of speech, the drinker said that the spectral coachman wore a three-cornered hat.

In 1994, a bus driver told me that the upper deck of a number 79 bus, which runs from Netherley to the city centre, is haunted by the ghost of an old man in a tweed cap and a mackintosh. Several drivers have glanced through the bus's periscope and seen the ghost sitting at the back of the bus on the upper deck. For some reason, the ghost prefers to appear when the bus goes through the Paddington area. The phantom passenger is thought to be the ghost of a man who died after falling from a bus some years ago.

Danny Hancock contacted me to tell me of a supernatural encounter on a 27 bus on Christmas Eve, 1994. Danny and his daughter boarded the bus at Paradise Street. They were the only passengers on the bus until an old man, aged about 70, got on the bus at Park Lane and sat behind them. Soon after, the man tapped Danny on the shoulder and he turned round and saw that the old man was holding out a chocolate Lion bar to his daughter. The daughter took the bar and Danny thanked him. After a few stops, Danny noticed that the old man had vanished. He had not passed him to get off the bus and the really strange thing was the chocolate bar's reality – Mr Hancock's daughter actually ate it!

# Liverpool Cathedral Ghosts

The myth still persists that ghosts are unholy and cannot enter a place of worship, despite the hundreds of well-documented cases of hauntings that have taken place in churches of every creed.

Perhaps the erroneous myth is fostered by the bad publicity ghosts receive from the sensational tabloids and the spate of films like *The Exorcist* and *Poltergeist*. In reality, amiable ghosts greatly outnumber malevolent ones and more and more psychical researchers are beginning to suspect that these so-called malevolent entities (such as poltergeists) are not real ghosts at all, merely the effects of an undiscovered type of energy that emanates from the mind of an overactive child.

So, if we accept that most ghosts are not the demonic monsters that Hollywood or the media paints them to be, it will not seem unusual if we hear of spectres roaming the aisles of churches and, occasionally, some of our great cathedrals, such as Liverpool's Anglican Cathedral, the largest in Britain. It took 74 years to build and was built on the site of a disused quarry. The quarry was abandoned in 1825 and left as a mini Grand Canyon. Filling in the used-up quarry was hardly feasible, so the old city fathers decided to convert the excavated area into a graveyard, which they called St James' Cemetery.

One warm August evening in 1973, a vagrant, Bob, woke up in the grounds of the cathedral's cemetery. He got to his feet and ran up a path that leads to the main gate and discovered, to his horror, that the gate was locked. He shouted to several passers-by, who stopped, but then walked on after surveying his ragged clothes and dirty appearance. Bob decided to try the other gate, at the other end of the cemetery. Rather reluctantly, he walked along a path that ran parallel to the rows of gravestones. Reaching the gate, he found that it, too, was locked, so he stood there with night falling fast. The vagrant shook the gate and shouted but the street outside was empty. He remembered seeing a gap in the railings on the eastern terrace of the cemetery and wandered off to check.

As Bob passed a huge domed circular monument in the centre of the cemetery, he paused to regain his breath, when he heard a noise echoing around him. In terror, he realised that the noise sounded like footsteps. Then Bob noticed the shady figure of a man wearing a long flowing cape and a top hat, walking, or rather limping, down the path towards him. Bob turned and fled up a slope. With the limping figure less than 30 feet away, he located the gap in the railings and squeezed through, scraping his chest and back and ran until he was back in the company of the living.

The domed temple, where Bob encountered the limping spectre, is the tomb of William Huskisson, who died from the horrific injuries he received when he fell under the wheels of George Stevenson's Rocket locomotive in September 1830. One of Huskisson's legs was badly crushed in the first ever recorded train accident. Could the limping apparition that Bob encountered be Huskisson's ghost?

****

At the other end of Hope Street stands the ultra-modern Metropolitan Cathedral. A ghost was seen here, in the early 1970s, by a group of tourists. They described the phantom as an indefinable figure that silently floated along the cathedral's main square before vanishing in front of their eyes. Other people who have spotted the ghost claim it is dressed in a monk's habit, but that description does not make sense.

There are no historical records of a monastery on the site of the cathedral. The last building to stand on the site presently occupied by the cathedral, was the infamous Liverpool Workhouse, where thousands of paupers laboured in inhuman conditions, to earn a piece of mouldy bread and a bowl of watery broth. It is possible that the ghost seen at the cathedral is not a spectral monk at all, but the ghost of one of the many destitute souls who perished in the cruel environment of the workhouse.

# Ghostly Maidens

After correlating and classifying the data amassed from the many interviews with witnesses who claim to have experienced uncanny encounters, I was surprised at the high number of people who had reported a particular type of apparition – the ghostly maiden.

Many mainstream psychologists would undoubtedly explain away the recurring tales of ghostly maidens by dismissing them as ancient archetypal desire-images, like the Lady of the Lake who features in the Arthurian romances, or the Homeric Sirens, or even the Irish and Scottish Banshee. However, the following two accounts seem to suggest the reality of spectral females that have an existence totally independent of Jung's collective unconscious.

In 1970, a 20-year-old man, Rob, met Jimmy, a friend he had not seen for years, at the Tudor nightclub in Parliament Street. The two men enjoyed a few drinks and, at 1.30 in the morning, Jimmy invited Rob back to his house in South Drive, Wavertree.

Jimmy's wife cooked the two men a fine supper and at about quarter to three, Rob said he felt tired and asked if he could sleep on the sofa. Jimmy said there was an old bed in his bedroom where could Rob sleep. The bed had been in the room when Jimmy and his wife had moved into the dwelling, which dated back to the 1850s. The couple got into their bed first and soon fell asleep. Rob got into the old bed at the other end of the long bedroom and fell into a deep, dreamless sleep.

Around 4 o'clock, something awakened Rob. He does not know whether it was a sound or something touching him, all he remembers is that something roused him from his slumber. The young man turned and glanced over at the bed where Jimmy and his wife were sleeping. What Rob saw over there sent a shiver down his spine. A young woman of around 18 was sitting on the couple's bed, eyeing Rob intensely. The ashen-faced girl just sat there staring directly at him without blinking. By the faint light of a street lamp that shone into the bedroom, Rob could see the silent girl's hair was raven black and long and that she was wearing an old-fashioned nightgown but what really unnerved him, were the girl's large, dark, lifeless eyes.

Rob ducked under the blankets for a few moments, then looked back at the bed. The sinister visitor was still there, still watching Rob with that blank expression that made his flesh creep. Again, he took refuge under the blankets. After a while, with sweat pouring from his brow, he reluctantly looked out and was horrified to see the ghostly maiden still sitting there, concentrating on him. Rob prayed for morning to come, expecting the girl to approach, but she never came. He dared not open his eyes and even managed to fall into an uneasy sleep.

In the morning, Rob told Jimmy about the girl but his friend just laughed and said he had been dreaming. Rob insisted that it had been real but Jimmy, knowing how superstitious his wife was, asked his friend not to mention the story to her. The girl's identity is not known but an old woman who lives in the area says that in the 1930s, a young woman died from meningitis in the house at South Drive where Rob stayed that night. The woman had a puritanical aunt who had kept her niece away from the opposite sex. Furthermore, the young woman died on her 18th birthday and she had long black hair and large brown eyes.

In Ferguson Road, West Derby, a young man experienced a similar phantom female in the late 1980s. The man was in bed when the figure of a long-haired woman, aged about 20, suddenly materialised in the room. Like the South Drive spectre, the apparition seemed to be intensely interested in the man and fixed her eyes (described as jet black) upon him for a long time. During it, the man experienced total paralysis and then the vision started to approach him. When it was just a couple of feet away, he managed to close his eyes. Instantly, the feeling of paralysis dissipated and, when he opened his eyes, the spectre was nowhere to be seen.

Surely the woman was just a sleep apparition? The man stresses that this was definitely not the case. This begs the question – who, or what, was the entity in his bedroom? The following possible answer may seem laughable but mediaeval demonologists maintained that 'succubi' – lustful female demons that seduce men – could easily assume human form, appearing as attractive women! Throughout history, there have been many recorded incidents of demonic-looking entities who have tried to seduce humans.

In the 17th century, in Moray Firth, an innocent young girl confessed to her parents that she had been seduced by a beautiful Adonis who often appeared in her bedroom after dark. When the parents broke into their daughter's room one night, having heard her talking to her mysterious lover, instead of a handsome young man, they were confronted by a hideous monster, who literally disappeared in a puff of smoke. Theologians hearing this strange tale conjectured that the passionate monster had been an incubus – a devil who forces sex upon women.

In this sceptical age, we do not accept superstitious interpretations. I am merely pointing out that bedroom intruders of a demonic kind are by no means a modern phenomenon. I recently received a distressed call from Anne, of Bootle, claiming her bedroom was haunted by an invisible entity that had patted her bottom and got into bed with her on numerous occasions. Looking into it, I decided the entity was something malevolent and sent a spiritualist with a good track record for removing such intruders to the woman's house and, up to now, she has not reported being harassed any further by the sinister being.

# The Story of Maureen Allen

There are many versions of this story but the following one – which comes from the north end of Liverpool – is the original.

In May 1866, Liverpool was hit by a cholera epidemic which killed hundreds, one of whom was Maureen Allen, a beautiful 16-year-old and the youngest member of a huge Irish family that had settled in Rose Place, Everton.

Maureen was laid in her coffin and the Irish wake, with its ritual drinking, feasting and lamentation went on all night long. On the evening of the wake, at about 7 o'clock, every member of the Allen family left the house to drown their sorrows in a pub near Great Homer Street.

At 8 o'clock, Richard O'Hare, an old friend of George Allen, the father of the dead girl, knocked on the front door of the empty home. O'Hare, unaware of Maureen Allen's death, was visiting from his home in Oliver Street, in the south end of the city.

O'Hare knocked several times but, after getting no answer, was about to turn away when one of the bedroom windows opened. O'Hare looked up and saw a pretty young red-haired girl leaning out of the window. He instantly recognised her as Maureen Allen.

"Hello, Maureen," he called, "is your father in?"

"No," answered Maureen, "nobody's in. They've all gone down the road to the pub".

O'Hare delved deep into his coat pocket and took out a couple of pennies, "here, Maureen," he said, "I have something for you".

"I can't," said Maureen, backing away from the window.

"Why?" asked O'Hare, puzzled.

"I can't open the door to anybody," she replied and closed her bedroom window.

O'Hare shook his head and headed for the pub where the Allen family was drinking. When he found George Allen, O'Hare told him about his conversation with Maureen but Allen stared at his friend angrily and grabbed him by the lapels of his jacket, telling him he thought the joke about Maureen was in bad taste. When O'Hare was told that Maureen had been dead for two days and was cold in her coffin, he trembled.

Later, back at the home of the Allen family, O'Hare saw that Maureen was laid out in her coffin.

"But I swear to God I saw Maureen at the window this very evening and she spoke to me," he insisted.

Upon hearing this, the four brothers of the dead girl attacked O'Hare and were about to throw him out of the house when their father intervened.

"Wait a moment!" shouted George Allen. "Leave him!"

Reluctantly, the four young men obeyed their father's instruction and let O'Hare go.

"What window did Maureen look at you from?" asked George Allen.

"The bedroom window directly above the front door."

"That'll be her bedroom," muttered Mrs Allen.

George Allen opened a door, revealing a small bedroom.

"Exactly. This was Maureen's bedroom," he said.

"Look at the curtains!" said Mrs Allen, "they're wide open. Yet I remember drawing the curtains in every room of the house".

"Are you sure you drew them?" asked one of her sons.

"Of course, I remember!" shouted Mrs Allen, "it's custom to do that when someone dies, or didn't you know?"

"Then just who did open the curtains in Maureen's room, then?"

"I told you, George," replied Richard O'Hare, "it was Maureen".

As O'Hare finished his sentence, a cold draught passed through the house.

# The Runcorn 'Thing'

Things that go bump in the night have quite a history. An entry in the famous diary of Samuel Pepys for Lord's Day, 5 February 1660, closes with the following…

"After supper, home; and before going to bed, I stood writing of this day its passages – while a drum came by, beating of a strange manner of beat, now and then a single stroke; which my wife and I wondered at, what the meaning of it should be."

Students of the paranormal believe that such inexplicable noises are the work of a poltergeist, which is a German word meaning noisy spirit.

A poltergeist quite often makes its debut by rapping or thumping the walls of the dwelling it has chosen to haunt, then it usually proceeds to move objects and furniture around. The early signs of the poltergeist's work – pens and keys that go missing – are often overlooked, or blamed on the mundane human trait of absent-mindedness.

In one case, a woman noticed all the pictures hanging on her living room wall were crooked. She corrected them, then went into the kitchen to make a cup of tea. When she returned to the living room, the pictures were all crooked again.

Minor disturbances like this may seem funny, but poltergeists can also do malevolent things. In 1979, a Berkshire pensioner living in a house plagued with poltergeist activity, received a serious head wound that required two stitches, after being struck by a small medicine cabinet which suddenly flew through the air.

The eerie forces of the invisible poltergeist seem to know no physical limitation. In 1713, a German doctor who made the mistake of taking a swipe at a poltergeist with his sword, narrowly missed being killed when his entire house was demolished by the unseen entity.

One of the best documented cases of a poltergeist outbreak in the North West occurred at Runcorn in 1952. It all began on the night of Sunday 10 August, when a scratching sound started to emanate from the drawer of a dressing-table in the bedroom of 1 Byron Street. Pensioner Sam Jones and his 17-year-old grandson, John Glynn, had only just got into bed when the scratching noise started. Suspecting a mouse, they got up to investigate but were baffled not to find any sign of a mouse in the drawer. They returned to their beds and settled down and, once again, the scratching started.

The following night, the dressing-table began to vibrate and rock about, accompanied by a succession of heavy thumps to the walls of the house. Not long afterwards, a clock shattered, as if struck by an invisible hammer and a blanket-chest, weighing half a hundredweight, rose into the air. Moments later, a water-jug smashed to smithereens.

News of the Byron Street poltergeist spread and the little home of Sam Jones was stormed by an army of the curious. Journalists, who knew a good story when they saw it, badgered old Sam and his grandson about every little detail.

The local police refused to believe that the source of the goings-on was not an earthly prankster and set traps for the mischief-maker. When these measures failed, Phil France, a spiritualist, was called in. After holding an exhausting three hour long seance in the haunted bedroom, he announced, "it is definitely a poltergeist".

The Reverend Stevens, a local Methodist minister, also investigated the case. During a vigil in the bedroom, he was hit on the head by a dictionary thrown by the unseen entity. He left immediately, declaring, "there is no question of this being a hoax!"

As the weeks went by, the poltergeist activity increased to such an extent that, by October, Sam Jones and his grandson found it impossible to sleep and had to move to a friend's house to avoid the nightly trauma. Around this time, a number of sinister events occurred. Three pedigree pigs on the Pool Farm, where Sam Jones worked, suddenly dropped dead. Five separate veterinary surgeons examined the dead animals but were at a loss as to the cause of for their mysterious deaths.

A fortnight later, the 53 other pigs on the farm also died for no known pathological reason. A couple of days after the last pig died, the farm's owner, Mr Crowther, saw a large black cloud, about seven feet in height, moving across his yard. The cloud was shapeless except for two prongs which stuck out of the back.

Three days later, Mr Crowther's wife witnessed the same cloud hovering over the farm. The most frightening encounter with the strange cloud happened a few weeks later, when Mr Crowther bumped into the gaseous apparition as he entered his kitchen. He was naturally scared and dashed to the light switch. On his way to the switch he brushed against the cloud, and the two prong-like protrusions attacked his throat! As Mr Crowther switched the kitchen light on, the cloud disintegrated.

One night, not long after that hair-raising meeting, Sam Jones visited Mr Crowther and asked him to witness the strange entity in the bedroom of Byron Street. Mr Crowther was understandably reluctant but decided to go to the house with Sam. When the two men bravely entered the bedroom, Mr Crowther was horrified to see the same forked cloud that had attacked him a few days ago, hovering menacingly over the bed. Moments later the cloud dissipated.

On 13 December 1952, Mr Crowther had his final encounter with the unearthly cloud. He was in his farmyard when the amorphous vapour appeared at his side. He noticed that it was smaller on this occasion and also lighter in colour. Suddenly, two of Mr Crowther's dogs charged at the cloud, barking and snarling.

The cloud retreated and rose about 18 feet into the air before disintegrating. Around this time, the poltergeist activity at Byron Street suddenly ended in a dramatic fashion. The carpet in the haunted bedroom suddenly tore itself from the floor and unseen hands seemed to be trying to fold it up. However, the poltergeist's departure came too late for poor John Glynn. He tried to put the incident behind him and joined the army but suffered a nervous breakdown and was subsequently discharged.

# The Ghosts of the Sky

Not all ghosts are the spirits of the deceased. There have been reports of apparitions of inanimate objects such as ships, cars, buses and even planes.

Over the years, many people in Speke have reported hearing the drone of a plane that sounds as if it has engine trouble. One night, when the mystery flyer was heard, several residents in Hunts Cross phoned Speke Airport to ask if a plane was in trouble but the air-traffic controllers were baffled, because their radar systems revealed no planes in their airspace. A local historian believes the ghost plane is the phantom of a German plane shot down over Liverpool during World War II.

In January 1974, the skies over Liverpool were visited by another aerial apparition – a black helicopter. The first reports came from policemen on night-duty and several other night-workers, who reported seeing a sinister black helicopter, without any lights, racing over the city's waterfront. The authorities quickly investigated the sightings, suspecting that the IRA was smuggling weapons into the country. Nightly vigils were held and patrols around the docks were set up but the unidentified chopper continued to traverse the airways. Several military helicopters were alleged to have pursued the mysterious helicopter unsuccessfully and, in a matter of months, the black helicopter left the skies for good without being identified.

Around the time of these sightings, another unidentified helicopter was buzzing the night skies of Cheshire and Derbyshire. A police spokesman involved in the hunt for the night flyer said that the pilot's flying skills were top class. Although flying at only 100 feet, the pilot managed to perform breathtaking aeronautical manoeuvres across a hilly terrain, that was criss-crossed with high-tension electricity lines.

On 16 January that year, the mystery pilot landed his helicopter in a field just west of Jodrell Bank and did not take off again for 90 minutes. Suggestions to use another chopper to pursue the mystery helicopter were dismissed by police chiefs as too hazardous and, a week later, the unknown helicopter pilot and his craft disappeared.

In May 1989, a massive search-and-rescue operation was launched, after scores of people in Crossens, Southport, reported seeing a Cessna light-aircraft come down in a nearby marsh. Police closed the Southport coastal road and emergency services searched the crash site but there was no trace of any aircraft wreckage.

At the same time, people on the other side of the Wirral Peninsula reported seeing an identical Cessna plane nose-diving into the River Dee. Thinking smugglers were dropping a consignment of drugs, the police swooped on the area to search for packages, but found nothing. Some think the plane seen crashing at Southport was the ghostly re-enactment of a pilot who had deliberately crashed his plane onto the beach in an act of suicide, when he was jilted by his girlfriend.

Another phantom plane has been seen flying along the Towys Valley between Llandeilo and Llandovery in Dyfed, Wales. The plane has been identified as a Wellington Bomber. In 1979, Martin Green, a writer who lives in the area, was walking along the A40 valley road when he noticed a huge dark plane heading towards him at tree-top level. The strange thing about the plane was that it was silent, even though its propellers were spinning. As the plane got nearer, Green could see that it was a Wellington and watched it fly overhead and into the distance. When he reached the local pub, he mentioned the sighting of the plane and several people said that they too had seen it – but none of them suspected that it was an apparition until Green decided to investigate.

He discovered that only one Wellington Bomber was still in existence in Britain, on permanent display in the RAF Museum in Hendon. Several weeks after Green's sighting, four other people saw the same silent plane flying across the valley and many have seen the apparition since then. Wellington Bombers did train over the Brecon Beacons and the Black Mountains, near to the Towys Valley, during the last war and it appears as if they are still flying there.

On Christmas Eve 1946, two Americans stationed at Burtonwood Airbase were returning to their billet after a night at a local pub, when they encountered a human-shaped cloud walking towards them. As it got closer, the two Americans saw that the figure was a headless airman. The spectral airman walked past the terrified men and into a hangar. The same headless ghost was seen again shortly afterwards by another military man and by a group of women who were returning from a dance at a nearby club. The ladies fled from the apparition, screaming!

The identity of the airman is thought to be that of a pilot decapitated when his plane crashed into a hanger at the airbase in 1944.

# The Ghost Family of Grove Street

One night in January 1980, a young woman, Susan, was walking down Grinfield Street in Edge Hill towards the Oxford public house, when she noticed the silhouetted figure of a woman walking in the field behind the pub. The woman was carrying a basket, had her hair tied up in a bun and wore a long, old-fashioned dress. As Susan looked, the woman glanced directly at her, turned round and started running towards St Stephen's Church at the top of Grove Street. Susan entered the pub and was about to tell a friend about the strange woman, when she overheard a man in the parlour talking about a woman he had seen in the field at the back of the pub in funny, greyish clothes. The man said that the woman kept stooping down, picking something up out of the grass and putting it in her basket. After glancing at his watch, he looked up and found that she had vanished.

The other drinkers in the pub just laughed and insisted that he was imagining things. The next day, out of curiosity, he inspected the part of the field where he had seen the grey figure and discovered clusters of toadstools amongst the grass there.

Grove Street's grey lady is not alone in her field. She shares it with 13 other apparitions. One, a diminutive flute-player who sits under an old oak tree in front of St Stephen's Church, has been seen and heard by people over the years and some swear that his appearance portends a streak of misfortune.

In the public house situated at the end of the haunted field, a man known for his honesty was in the pub's empty parlour one night, when he noticed a small, old man wearing a trilby and raincoat and a girl about 12-years-old, sitting at a table. The pair sat there for a few moments with expressionless faces – then vanished.

Towards the end of Grove Street, in Cambridge Street, late-night revellers have reportedly heard the sound of hooves. The invisible steed is said to gallop from the grounds of the University to Lully Street, where the sound comes to an abrupt halt. In February 1975, a field adjacent to Lully Street became the setting for a sinister spectacle that was witnessed by residents in a nearby block of flats. At about 12.45 am, a couple, getting ready for bed, noticed the glow of a fire in the centre of the field facing their flat.

At first, they thought that someone was burning rubbish but then they noticed nine extremely large black cats sitting in a perfect circle around the fire. Within a few minutes, bedroom windows were opening all over the block of flats and bemused faces looked down at the strange circle. Then, at 1 o'clock, the fire in the field rapidly dimmed to a faint ember and the black cats could no longer be seen.

Why Grove Street should have an abundance of spectres is unknown. Recently, another unexplained incident – reported in the *Liverpool Echo* – occurred in the same area.

In 1988, two policemen came across an old, expensively-made coffin, in a car park at the top of Grove Street. The police were relieved to find that the velvet-lined coffin was empty but were obviously perplexed at finding it in the middle of a car park. The coffin was later deposited in the lost property room of Admiral Street Police Station. As yet, no dawn-fearing vampire or weary zombie has turned up to collect it.

# Devon Street's Reformed Gambler

For many years I have tried to track down the originator of the following tale. Many people, particularly in the north end of Liverpool, have heard about a ragman who had a supernatural experience in Elizabeth Street, Edge Hill, early this century, but the origin of the story is a mystery.

Most people I have talked to claim that the incident occurred in the autumn of 1901. This consensus sent shivers down my spine, because my grandmother mentioned that year when she told me the tale of a rag and bone man called John Irving.

Late one afternoon in November 1901, John Irving pushed his old hand-cart out of the backyard of his home in Devon Street and threaded his way through the alleyways that led out onto the cobbled roads crying, "any old rags?" Irving was a notorious gambler who had a habit of squandering his meagre earnings on cards, drink and horse-racing, instead of supporting his wife and family. On the rare occasions when his gambling paid off, he would go missing for days, often returning home in a drunken and violent state. His wife, a timid, uncomplaining woman never deserted him, however.

At about 4.30 in the afternoon, a dense fog rolled in from the Mersey and Irving dropped the handles of his hand-cart and pulled up his collar to keep the chill out. As he did so, he thought he heard footsteps behind him. He turned round and peered into the swirling fog, waiting for someone to emerge. The footsteps got louder, then ceased and the dark outline of a stationary dog became visible. Irving shuddered. The dog, which was black and of an indeterminable breed, seemed to have a human-like face.

"Go on, shoo!" Irving shouted at the sinister-looking hound but the dog stayed where it was and its peculiar face seemed to grin. The ragman grabbed the handles of his hand-cart and moved off slowly through the lonely, foggy street, afraid to look back. Moments later, the sound of approaching footsteps resumed.

Irving was halfway up the street, contemplating whether he should make a run for it, when the roar of a fog-horn blasted through the air. The ragman's heart pounded when, as the echo of the fog-horn died away, the thudding footsteps could still be heard. Irving let go of his hand-cart, ran to the nearest house and hammered on the front door. He then waited anxiously, expecting the eerie dog to approach but it was nowhere to be seen. The front door of the house creaked open slightly and an old maid peered out at the ragman.

"Er, would the master of the house have any old garments or the like that he wants to be rid of?" Irving asked, removing his cap.

"At this hour? Come back tomorrow," snapped the old maid, haughtily.

"Please," Irving begged, clutching his cap over his heart, "my wife is ill and I have no money to buy her medicine".

After a long silent pause, the maid said, "wait there a moment," and closed the door. Irving waited nervously. The fog was getting thicker and the street was as quiet as the grave. The front door of the house suddenly opened again, startling him.

"Come in," said the maid.

"Thank you," replied Irving, stepping into the house.

The maid led him down a long, dimly-lit hallway and into the parlour, where an old grey-haired woman with a hawk-like nose was sitting at a sewing table, engrossed in her embroidery. She looked up at Irving and smiled.

"Good evening, ma'am."

"Good evening. Looks like a pea-souper out there!" she remarked.

"It is, yes. Fog's thick enough to cut with a knife," replied Irving, eyeing the room up.

"Fetch the cast-offs, Margaret," the woman ordered, then turned to Irving and said, "pull a chair over to the fire, you look frozen".

"Thanks, ma'am, you're very considerate."

Irving positioned a heavy mahogany chair, that was standing in a corner, in front of the blazing coal fire.

"There, finished!" exclaimed the woman, surveying her completed needlework.

"Very nice, ma'am," praised the ragman, leaning over to inspect the embroidered image of a rose, "never seen anything as lifelike. You must be an artist".

The old woman laughed, lifted the lid of the sewing table and placed her embroidery, needles, pin-cushion and thimble inside one of its compartments. She then surprised Irving by taking out a pack of cards from the compartment.

"My late husband's," she explained, staring at the pack, "how we whiled away the long hours of a winter evening with a game of whist".

"I indulge in a game myself, from time to time," admitted Irving, "I don't make it a habit, of course".

"Really? That is a coincidence. If you wish, we could enjoy a game of whist until the maid returns," suggested the woman, removing the cards from their box.

"Er, whist is a bit too highfalutin' for me, ma'am. Poker's my game," said Irving, awkwardly.

"Then poker it is!" declared the woman, shuffling the cards.

After the first game, she pointed over to a cabinet.

"Have a drink."

Irving walked over to the cabinet and pulled its doors open. His eyes widened at the sight of bottles of whisky, gin, port and rum. The ragman grabbed a glass and poured himself a generous measure of the latter.

"Bring the bottle over to the table, if you wish," said the woman, "I'm a teetotaller. My husband was the tippler".

The hours flew by, until the clock on the mantelpiece started chiming as it struck midnight.

"Is that the time?" exclaimed the ragman, "I'd better be going!"

"Just one more game," pleaded the woman, "you've won every game tonight. I must win the last one".

Although he was thoroughly intoxicated, the ragman felt uneasy. There was something wrong.

"The maid's taking her time, isn't she?" he asked suspiciously.

"She'll be down in a moment. Sit down and deal, please. I won't feel right letting you out into the fog in that state."

Irving gathered the cards.

"Alright. One more game, but then I'm off."

As the ragman shuffled the pack, a card fell to the floor. He bent down to search for it. It was not under the table, so then he looked under the woman's chair.

"No! Leave it!" snapped the woman, agitated.

Irving suddenly noticed the corner of the card, protruding from the bottom of the woman's ankle-length dress. He dared to lift the dress from the floor a couple of inches, in order to grab the card. On doing this, he realised that she did not have human feet, she had hooves – like the devil. The shock of this revelation made him faint.

When he came to, he found himself in a dark, derelict house. Getting to his feet, he ran over the bare floorboards and out into the hall and tried to open the front door. The wood of the door-frame was in such a rotten state that the door fell on top of him but he suffered nothing worse than a bruised arm. His cart was outside the house but he decided to leave it and ran home to Devon Street in a sorry state.

John Irving became a reformed man overnight. He shuddered at the sight of a poker game, became a teetotal family man and attended church every Sunday thereafter.

# The Peeping Tom

The following story was investigated by a paranormal research group based in Hunts Cross and it concerns a creepy peeping tom who abuses his unusual psychic talent. Beware, this sinister voyeur is still active!

For centuries, mystics and occultists have claimed that each of us has a spirit-like entity, called the astral body, stowed away in our physical body. This astral body is said to contain the soul, the consciousness and the 'third eye'. It is thought that some people can project their astral body out of their physical body and view things which are happening miles away. Out-of-body experiences are also thought to take place when a person is in bad health or near death. However, according to many yogis and mystics, we can all project ourselves out of our bodies with regular practise at meditation but it is thought to be a very dangerous exercise – there are reports of some people being unable to get back into their bodies after projecting from them.

If you think that all these claims about an astral body are bunkum, think again, because the CIA, FBI and several police forces in the United States and Europe have admitted that they are employing so-called, 'remote viewers' – experts who know how to project their consciousness out of their bodies so that they can view events taking place anywhere in the world. The CIA has admitted using remote viewers to spy on nuclear missile installations in the heart of the old Soviet Union and even NASA has admitted that they have employed remote viewers to see if they can find out data on other planets. Remote viewers have even been used successfully by police to locate the bodies of murder victims and missing people.

There is also said to be a remote viewer living in the Liverpool area who is allegedly abusing his psychic ability, in order to spy on women in their homes and workplaces. For legal reasons, he cannot be named but paranormal investigators claim to know his identity. We'll call him Russell.

In August 1997, Josephine, who works for a chemists in the city, was enjoying a lunchtime meal at Wetherspoons, a large pub in Charlotte Row, when a small, middle-aged man, wearing yellow-tinted spectacles, came over and said, "Hi, Jo!"

Jo stopped eating and asked, "who are you?"

"Russell," he replied, with a sinister sneer and sat opposite at the table.

"I'm sorry, I don't know you," said Jo uneasily.

"I know you don't know me – but I know you," retorted Russell.

"What do you mean?" replied Jo, feeling intimidated by the stranger.

"I saw you cutting your toenails on your bed last night, just after you got out the bath. You shouldn't use your fellah's razor to shave your legs, y'know. He has to use that razor himself."

"Are you some sort of pervert? I'm gonna call the police now," Jo declared furiously.

"Calm down, Jo. You read too much Stephen King. You're up to page fifty-six of his latest book, aren't you? I visit you every night and you can't see me. I've even seen your little birthmark."

Russell described the exact location of the birthmark on a very private part of Jo's anatomy. Jo snapped and threw a butter knife at Russell. Then, as one of the staff came over to see what was going on, Russell ran out of the pub, laughing. Jo did not know what to think. She wondered if Russell was watching her with binoculars, or a telescope, from the block of flats facing her home. Two years ago, Jo's friend had spotted a man in those flats looking at her with an enormous reflector telescope but Jo knew that a peeping tom with a telescope could not see into her bathroom, or behind the drawn curtains of her bedroom. She mentioned the creepy incident to her friends at work and they advised her to contact a group of paranormal investigators who had recently been featured on local radio.

The investigators told Jo that they knew of an 18-year-old girl in Liverpool who was also getting strange phonecalls and letters from a guy who said he could visit her in his astral body. The pest had said his name was Russell. The research group said that they could not do anything about the psychic peeping tom and advised her to move to another area.

Jo convinced her boyfriend she wanted to move to a flat near Sefton Park and he reluctantly agreed. However, the move made no difference; Jo was still under supernatural surveillance. A week later, she was in a shop in Bold Street when she felt a tap her on the shoulder. It was Russell.

Jo was dumbfounded as the stalker remarked, "your other flat was better. The place you're in now is facing away from the park. Isn't that Mrs Davies a nosey old neighbour?" Russell added, "she puts a glass against the wall and listens to you and your fellah – especially when you two make love".

"That's it, I'm going to the police," snapped Jo, "there are cameras in this store taping you right now, so they'll know what you look like".

Russell giggled.

"hey, your fellah isn't very adventurous between the sheets, is he?"

At this Jo lost her cool and picked up a pan and whacked Russell.

"You nutter!" he yelled as ran out the store.

At work the next day, Jo's friend, Lisa, confronted her.

"You're a real two-faced, gossiping, little backstabber."

"What are you talking about?" asked Jo, baffled.

"You know what I'm talking about," Lisa replied, "I got a phone call from this fellah last night and he said you and your fellah were slagging me off and saying I slept with three different men behind my boyfriend's back."

"Who told you this, Lisa?" asked Jo, her face going red.

"Russell, this fellah who said he knows you," Lisa replied taking a swipe at Jo.

A fight ensued and both girls ended up dragging each other around the shop by the hair, until a supervisor and a customer intervened.

When Jo returned home, she started to cry. She *had* said all those things about her friend Lisa and talked about her to her boyfriend but had forgotten about the accursed eavesdropper, Russell. Unfortunately, this story has no pleasant ending because Russell is, by all accounts, still roaming about the city and spying on women. So cover yourself up tonight and be careful what you say about your friends ... because someone might be listening ...

# The Ghost that Cased Joints

The following tale is bizarre but is catalogued in the annals of the Psychical Research Society in London. The incident allegedly happened in Liverpool in the 1950s.

In 1951, a burglar broke into an office in Speke, opened the safe, and stole about £900. The police were baffled, it looked like an inside job, for the thief had evidently known the combination of the safe. The police forensic officer managed to extract part of one thumbprint on the safe door. The next evening, again in Speke, a post office was broken into and the safe opened by someone who knew the combination. This time, £1000 was taken. Police uncovered a thumb and fingerprint on the door and matched the print to that on the office safe. The following week, a thief broke into the premises of a betting shop in Halewood and emptied the safe, which was hidden in the concrete floor under a desk. The fingerprints on the desk matched the prints at the other crime scene but the police were baffled at the burglar's modus operandi; how did he know the combinations of the safes?

The case took a bizarre twist when a young lady who had been a counter clerk at the burgled post office, was being cross-questioned by two detectives. She was asked to go through all the trivial events of her working day, when she suddenly said, "oh yes! The ghost".

The slightly bemused detectives asked her to explain what she meant and she gave her account of what she had seen.

"I came in earlier than usual and when I went to the back room where the safe was, I saw this ghastly face, white, with a thick black moustache. It seemed to come through the wall, high up in the corner, near the ceiling and it was looking at me with a surprised look. Within a blink it was gone and I thought I'd been seeing things."

The counter clerk had told no one about the weird experience because she feared being dismissed by her boss. The detectives promised the woman they would say nothing about her eerie encounter.

A week later, a clerk who had stayed behind at Martins Bank in Liverpool, to sort out the accounts of a local company, was startled to see the face of a man in the darkness behind him. The clerk swung his desk lamp up and shone it at the intruder, only to find that the face had disappeared. The bank clerk remembered, however, that the face had a thick black moustache. That evening, someone broke into the bank with a crowbar, bypassed the alarm by inserting a disabling key that had been hidden under a ledger and opened the safe. This time, a policeman on his beat entered the bank and collared the robber. The thief turned out to be George Johnson, a small-time pickpocket, originally from Preston.

When Johnson was interrogated, he confessed to being responsible for the spate of safe robberies but when he told the police how he had known the combinations to the safes and other details, the detectives thought he must either be insane, or else pretending to be mad.

Johnson said the ghost of his recently-deceased partner-in-crime, Arthur Hennessy, had acted as his accomplice. Johnson explained that he was of Romany stock and was psychic, this ability enabling him to communicate with the ghost of his close mate who had died recently in a car crash. The ghost cased the joints and came back to tell him the combinations and where the safes were hidden. Police refused to believe Johnson's odd tale but when they showed a photograph of his dead friend to the bank clerk and the post office counter clerk, the two witnesses agreed the face was identical to the ghostly face they had seen. The case took another twist, a week later, when George Johnson suffered a very heavy nosebleed, dying minutes later, apparently from natural causes.

No one was tried for the baffling safe robberies and the crimes ceased upon Johnson's death. Police gave little publicity to the case – for which they had no rational explanation to offer.

# A Picture of Evil

Early in March 1995, a young couple, Denise and Joe, moved into a house in Liverpool. The house dated back to early Victorian times and had a welcoming atmosphere with a lovely panoramic view of the river from an upstairs window.

A fortnight after they had moved in, the couple heard strange noises coming from the attic. Denise was naturally scared but Joe pointed out that it was probably just the wind rattling the windows and he went up with a torch, just to make sure. He was right, the wind was rattling the loose frame of the skylight; there was nothing ghostly about the sounds after all. Denise came up into the attic and Joe remarked, "God, this place has a real musky smell."

Noticing a large wooden tea-chest, Denise grabbed the torch and, aiming at the chest, opened it. The box contained bundles of cobwebbed documents and two pictures framed with ornate gold borders. One was of a slim man, about 30, with dark hair and a Van Dyck beard, the other was of a plump-looking woman with honey-blonde hair and a cheerful, rosy-cheeked face. As Denise shone the torch at these paintings, the attic door burst open and a terrific howling sound, like a gale-force wind, whistled through the doorway. The door then slammed shut with such a force that dust and loose plaster fell from the ceiling of the attic. Denise trembled and Joe hugged her reassuringly.

"It's okay, Denise; it was just a draught."

Denise swore.

"That was not a draught! Let's get out of here."

She dropped the paintings back in the large tea-chest and left the attic.

In bed that night, Joe was soon asleep but Denise lay awake, startled by a distinctive creaking noise, the sound of a floorboard outside the bedroom door. She peered over the duvet, staring in horror as the handle of the bedroom door twisted and the door slowly opened a few inches. She screamed and shook Joe awake.

"Someone's outside on the landing. They opened the door," she gasped.

"Don't go!" Denise pleaded as Joe went over to the door and peeped outside. He looked both ways but there was only darkness. However, he did notice a peculiar musky smell. Assuming that the gales outside had opened the door, he grumpily returned to bed.

A few days later, when Joe was at work, she was lying in bed with influenza. Feeling really ill, she tried to read a book but, around three in the afternoon, something weird began to happen. Denise heard the faint sounds of music coming from somewhere nearby. She put the book down on the floor and listened to the faint strains of a harpsichord. Suddenly, a strange darkness came over the room. All light from the bedroom window seemed to fade, as if a black cloud had descended on the house, so dark she had to switch on the bedside lamp. To her horror she heard the floorboard creak outside her bedroom door. At that precise moment, the bedside lamp went out with a clinking sound, as if the bulb had gone.

Denise felt fear course through her body. She sat up in bed, staring at the bedroom door, as the handle began to turn, just as it had done the other night. She felt her heart pounding as the door creaked open, wider and wider.

As the figure entered the room, Denise recognised him immediately as the man depicted in the oil painting in the attic. He had straight black, shoulder-length hair, dark menacing eyes with thick eyebrows, a Van Dyck beard and he wore a black velvet coat with white cuffs. She was so afraid, she could not speak.

The stranger's teeth were yellow and crooked. In a refined voice he whispered, "hello, Miss." He walked across the room and leaned over Denise. Terrified, she could not turn away. The man's dark eyes seemed to have a hypnotic pull on her. She noticed the dank, musky smell he gave off, the same odour of decay that had greeted her when she had opened the large tea-chest in the attic. The stranger stooped down and kissed Denise's face. She trembled as his ice-cold face pressed against hers, his beard and moustache bristling against her cheeks as he caressed her. Suddenly, the intruder announced, "oh, to be alive again, that would be something," and he kissed and bit her neck. Denise suddenly regained the power to move and, picking up the bedside lamp, tried to hit her attacker on the head with it.

The stranger looked up, his eyes glaring with a look of pure evil. He clenched his crooked teeth and snarled, "don't you dare!"

At that moment, the doorbell rang out and the startled stranger, fled from the bedroom in one swift movement, like a shadow. Denise ran out of the bedroom in her nightdress and almost fell down the stairs. She opened the door and saw, to her relief, that it was Joe, who had been sent home because he, too, seemed to be coming down with the flu.

When Joe saw the state Denise was in – and the large lovebite on her neck, he became concerned.

"Denise? What's going on?" he demanded.

Denise gave him a blow-by-blow account of the assault and said she was leaving the house that very moment. Joe persuaded her to stay and phoned the police. Having searched the house thoroughly to find there was no stranger on the premises, the police suggested that Denise had a high temperature and had probably hallucinated the whole incident.

"Then who did this then?" She screamed and pointed to the red lovebite on her neck.

The police said nothing but one of the officers glanced at Joe and smiled.

"I didn't do it," Joe assured him and watched the policemen leave.

That evening, Joe and two of his friends searched the house again. One of his mates, Alex, opened the tea-chest and looked at the paintings.

"What are these?" he asked.

Joe recalled that Denise had told him that the attacker looked exactly like the man in the painting.

"One's of some weird-looking fellow and the other's of a woman."

"No, this one's blank," Alex replied and showed the painting to Joe.

It was just a dark green background. The man with the Van Dyck beard had vanished from the painting. Joe tried to rationalise this bizarre occurrence and wondered if fungus had recently corrupted the painting but he knew that was impossible. On the back of the painting, a label with faded writing said, 'Richard Brownrigg, musician'.

Joe remembered that Denise had heard the eerie harpsichord music before the man came into her bedroom and, that night, the couple left to live with her parents until they found accommodation in another area of the city. The house where they lived is still said to be haunted, according to the present residents, who are not aware of the weird paintings in the attic. Recently, at 2 o'clock in the morning, the faces of a dark, bearded man and a blonde woman were seen staring out of a second storey window …

# Bernie with the Broken Neck

This incident allegedly took place shortly before Christmas, one snowy night in the 1970s. It was one in the morning and Brownlow Hill was deserted. A light snow was falling and settling on the ground but one person who was out at that hour seemed unaffected by the chilly weather. Mr Smith, a Liverpool businessman, walked up the flights of steps in Brownlow Hill that led to the Metropolitan Cathedral's main square. As he reached the top of the icy steps, his footsteps echoed in the silence.

The businessman stopped in his tracks and took out his keys. He held the keyring given to him by his wife just three years ago. Mr Smith had stopped at the very place where he and Melanie had walked on the night of their first date. He had met her at the Augustus John pub; they had both been students at Liverpool University. He had always been sceptical about true love until he met Melanie. She had moved into his flat and they married less than a year later. Tragedy closely followed, when Melanie died from a brain tumour and it hurt Mr Smith to think of his wife's suffering. Unable to come to terms with her loss, he found himself on this freezing December morning at the very spot where he had once been so happy.

Mr Smith climbed onto the snow-covered wall that bordered the square and prepared himself to jump down into the crypt, some 50 feet below. Life was unbearable without Melanie, he could not spend another Christmas without her. He closed his eyes and was about to jump when someone shouted out behind him. He looked around in surprise, having thought he was alone.

"Don't!" shouted a scruffy-looking man standing in the square behind him. He held out his arms to the would-be suicide.

"Shut up! Beat it!" Mr Smith warned him and started to cry.

The tramp stood his ground.

"No, I won't. It isn't right. Just because your little world is falling apart. That's the coward's way out!"

Mr Smith shouted a string of four-letter words and ended, "I don't want to live, so just leave me alone."

"Okay, friend, but have you ever wondered what will become of you if you do decide to jump?"

"Yes," said Mr Smith, "I'll be dead, that's what'll become of me."

"A child knows that," persisted the tramp, "but what if that isn't the end?"

"You're drunk, just leave me alone," snapped Smith and he turned back to look at the glistening ground below.

"You mightn't even die if you fall down there," the tramp chuckled.

"Just go, will you?"

The tramp stayed put and rambled on, "you could smash your head in and end up like a cabbage. You'll have to be spoon-fed."

Mr Smith took a deep breath and started to sway back and forth slightly.

"Even if you smash your brains in and your organs fly everywhere, you might still take a few minutes to die," added the tramp, "and you know when you're lying there after the fall and you're barely alive, all your organs are ruptured and your blood is spreading into a great big puddle, you taste your own salty blood in your mouth and you are seized by this terrible panic and you change your mind and suddenly want to live. You hope and wish that it's all just a bad dream but it isn't; you realise with horror that you're going to die."

"And how do you know all this?" Mr Smith asked the tramp, diverted from his own misery.

"I'll give you a clue," grinned the tramp and tilted his head until his ear touched his shoulder.

Mr Smith shuddered when he saw the tramp's contortion act. Surely he was just double-jointed. The tramp then flipped his head right back in one swift movement, so the back of his head touched his shoulder blades. With a sense of mounting horror, Mr Smith realised that no one – even someone double-jointed – could flip his head back like that. The tramp turned around on the spot and his dangling head swung about as if his neck was broken.

With his face upside down, he smiled, "I jumped. Look what happened."

Mr Smith got down off the wall, trembling, and ran across the square in a state of fright. He turned back once and saw that the tramp had vanished. The businessman hesitated and looked in the snow. He could see his trail of footprints but could see no trace of footprints leading to the spot where the vagrant had appeared. Mr Smith hurried down the stairs and raced up Brownlow Hill. It had stopped snowing and a full moon had emerged from a break in the clouds. Mr Smith glanced back towards the Cathedral and saw a solitary shadowy figure coming down the steps in the moonlight. He could not be sure, but the figure looked like the tramp with the broken neck. Horrified, he realised it was heading his way. He was relieved to see a black hackney cab and the taxi took him safely to his home in Old Swan.

The chilling experience left Mr Smith with no further desires to end his life and he gradually pulled himself out of his depression. In the February of the following year, he read an interesting article in the *Liverpool Echo* that reported a group of tourists visiting the Metropolitan Cathedral had encountered the ghost of a shabby-looking man in the Cathedral's main square. After smiling at the Americans, the man vanished before their startled eyes. A ghosthunter looked into the case and found that many other people had seen the same solid-looking phantom of a bedraggled figure. A medium who was brought in to make contact with the ghost, claimed the apparition was Bernie Brown, who had died in the Liverpool Workhouse in the 19th century after breaking his neck jumping from a window. This seemed to fit, because the Cathedral was built on the site of the old Liverpool Workhouse. So if you're travelling near Brownlow Hill tonight … watch out for Bernie with the broken neck.

# The Harrington School Visions

The German writer, Goethe, once asserted that an evil or tragic event sometimes gives a warning of its approach by casting its shadow ahead of its path. Goethe was talking about premonitions – supernatural warnings of a dire future event which may take the form of a hunch, a nightmare, or even a vision – as I will recount later in this chapter. Scientists say that, by all rational criteria, premonitions are impossible, because the future has yet to take place, but there have been well-documented instances of premonitions that are hard to explain with our present scientific knowledge. One example occurred on 20 April 1889, when a young Austrian, Klara, went into labour.

The old midwife who attended Klara had delivered countless babies but when she delivered Klara's baby, she felt clumsy and experienced a strange icy feeling in her hands. She thought it must be her circulation but when the baby started to appear, she began to tremble and her teeth started to chatter. The midwife had an overwhelming sensation that something terrible was going to happen, experiencing what would now be labelled as a panic attack. She cut the cord and successfully delivered the child and, later, the sense of touch returned to her numb hands. However, for months afterwards she suffered terrible bouts of depression and even contemplated suicide. Why the midwife took such a strange turn is not known but, perhaps, it was something to do with the fact that the new-born infant she had delivered was Adolf Hitler.

Another example of a chilling premonition happened here in Liverpool. The case is known as the Harrington School Visions. At midday on 7 June 1926, Peter Kelly, a schoolboy, told a friend he had just seen something terrifying staring at him from a window in Harrington School, in Stanhope Street. Peter had almost fallen off his bicycle after seeing a grotesque skull gazing down at him from the school window. His mate was naturally sceptical but asked Peter to show him what he had seen. When the boys arrived at the school, a young woman was standing on the pavement, staring up at the windows of the building. She too had noticed the skull, which looked as if it was screaming. The boys noticed that all around the apparition were flames, which seemed to be consuming its grotesque face. The lady on the pavement screamed, threw her hands to her face and ran home to tell her family of the strange vision.

Crowds were soon swarming around the school, waiting for the vision to reappear. The thrillseekers were not disappointed. The ghostly face of an old woman materialised, wringing her hands and shaking her head. Superstitious members of the crowd made the sign of the cross and a gang of men who had been demolishing a house nearby, stopped work to see what was going on and witnessed a gallery of eerie faces appear in the windows. A man stared out with his hair on fire and in terrible pain before the flames scorched his face, turning it black, so that only his teeth and the whites of his eyes could be seen. The other faces were of children and, as the flames quickly obscured their heads, many in the crowd fainted or turned away in horror.

The fire brigade arrived as people had assumed that there must be a fire raging but there was no smoke coming from the building. When the firemen hammered on the school door, a janitor answered. He said he had just checked and there was no fire. The firemen went to the floor where the faces had been seen but found the classrooms deserted.

The *Liverpool Echo* and other newspapers reported the strange story claiming that it had been a case of mass hysteria and conjectured that the incident had probably been caused by reflections in the school windows. The janitor claimed he knew the truth but the journalists did not bother to interview him. The janitor knew that the glass panes which the burning faces had peered through, had been salvaged from a house in Edge Hill. The house had been destroyed in a blaze which had claimed the lives of a large family. The firefighters had witnessed the victims of the blaze, young and old, screaming at the windows as the smoke overcame them and the flames roasted them alive. An unscrupulous glazier later took many of the the intact glass panes from the burnt-out house and used them in Harrington School. The janitor believed that the faces of the blaze victims had somehow been absorbed into the window panes. His theory was way ahead of its time; this was years before holographic images were stored on glass plates by a laser.

But it seems the Harrington School faces might have been a premonition because, one year later, the janitor and his family were burnt alive when a fire broke out in their home. Witnesses of the blaze said he appeared at the window, trying to open it, but the flames rose up and burnt his hair. Within seconds, his face had turned black with the smoke and fire. The janitor, his four children and his old mother, all died in the tragic blaze.

# Another Girl

At a semi-detached house in Tuebrook, in 1996, a young couple, Tony and Susan, were watching television one night. At a quarter to ten, the couple's little Jack Russell dog, Judy, came in and looked at Susan, wanting to go out. Susan put on her sandals, grabbed her coat, and put the lead on Judy. She walked around the roads of the neighbourhood for about 20 minutes. When she returned to her house, she tip-toed through the garden and spied on Tony through the living-room window to see if he was having a cigarette – he had quit smoking for almost a week – but as she peered through the window, she was stunned by what she saw.

Sitting on the sofa was a red-haired young woman wearing nothing but a revealing negligee and black lacy underwear. The stranger was dipping a spoon into a small tub of ice cream as she watched the television, seemingly unaware of Susan. Susan's heart skipped a beat. Who was the girl on the sofa? She certainly intended to find out and stormed to the front door and hammered on the knocker.

After almost a minute, Tony came down complaining, "I was on the toilet! Don't tell me; you forgot your key again."

Susan pushed her boyfriend aside and let go of the leash. She went into the living room demanding to know what was going on but there was no girl there. Just the television set blaring out to an empty living-room.

"What's up?" Tony asked, watching his girlfriend pulling the curtains back, as if she was looking for someone.

Susan was naturally confused and told Tony about the girl she had seen in their living room. Tony shook his head and laughed nervously.

"You've been looking through next door's window. That girl next door, Stacey, she's got red hair."

"I looked through *this* window. This one! And the girl next door has brown hair and she's only fifteen. She was nothing like the girl I saw; her hair was red, and she looked about twenty-five."

Tony sat Susan down and hugged her, joking.

"Unless it was a ghost!"

"Don't be talking about things like that at this time of night," Susan shivered, "it was really weird. She looked so real. She was eating ice cream."

Next day, Tony went for a job interview at the Albert Dock as a barman at one of the pubs there. Later that afternoon, Susan returned home from college and while she was making herself a cup of tea, heard the gate outside clang shut. She assumed it was Tony returning from his interview but, when she looked out of the window, she was astonished to see that it the mysterious red-head she had seen sitting on her sofa. The woman was walking down the path towards the house. Susan braced herself.

"That Tony has been seeing someone else. I knew it."

Susan waited tensely for the girl to knock but was surprised to hear a key rattle in the lock. The door opened and footsteps sounded on the stairs. Putting down her tea, Susan followed to confront her rival but the upstairs rooms were empty. Then something even more bizarre happened. Susan walked into the empty room where Tony stored all his football programmes and sports books. The room had been transformed into a nursery and a baby was crying in a cot in the corner of the room.

Susan felt dizzy with the shock. The front door opened and Tony shouted, "Sue! I got the job! I start Monday!"

Susan came downstairs.

"Whose is that baby upstairs? What the hell is going on?" she asked him.

Tony followed her upstairs. When he looked into the box room, all that was to be seen was his old piles of books and football memorabilia. Susan put her hands to her face, "Tony, I think I should see a doctor. I'm going mad. I saw a baby in a cot in here and that red-haired girl again, she came into the house."

A week later, Susan was alone in the house and went upstairs to the bathroom. Looking in the mirror, she noticed something pass the bathroom doorway behind her. It looked like a fleeting glimpse of the red-haired girl. As She recovered from the fright, she heard an American voice come from the bedroom saying, "hi, Lauren! Mommy's come to change your diaper."

Susan heard a baby babbling and went into each room but found them empty.

Running downstairs, she phoned the pub where Tony was working and begged him to come home at once. Soon after, Tony was sitting on the sofa with his girlfriend, very concerned about the state of her mind. Then he too heard something that defied explanation. A radio came on upstairs, even though Tony knew there was no radio upstairs. A rock song boomed out at full volume, followed by the voice of a girl with an American accent shouting, "turn that down, Tony."

The song sounded just like a number by the rock band, Oasis, but Tony, a fan of the group, had never heard it before. The sounds faded away and Tony went upstairs with Susan but there was no one about and no radio to be seen anywhere.

The biggest shock came the following Sunday morning. Susan came downstairs and smelt a strange, sweet aroma, the scent of flowers, emanating from the front room. On entering the room, She almost had a heart attack when she saw an open coffin on a stand, with wreaths and other floral tributes around it. In the coffin was her own body.

Susan ran screaming up the stairs and threw herself at Tony. He began to tremble and said it had just been a bad dream but he, too, could smell flowers. Yet when he went downstairs, he found the room empty.

A fortnight later, Susan was tragically knocked down and killed whilst visiting her cousin in Warrington. Before the funeral, her body was brought home and laid to rest in her coffin in the front room.

In November 1996, Tony met a red-haired American student who was staying in Britain. The girl is currently living with him, helping him to get over the loss of Susan. Recently, she discovered she was pregnant and the couple plan to call the baby Lauren, if it's a girl. Tony has already cleared out his boxroom and converted it into a nursery, just as Susan had foreseen a year before. When Tony heard Oasis bring out a single, *Stand By Me*, he shuddered, recalling that that was the song he had heard blaring out from the upstairs radio. It was as if Tony and Susan had been seeing and hearing sneak previews of Tony's future life – with another girl.

# Phantoms of the Living

According to recent research in the UK, Europe and the United States, a staggering 45% of all ghost sightings are actually encounters with phantasms of the living; phantom images of people who are in perfect health. Unlike the mysterious doppelganger – a sinister, solid-looking twin of a person who is often (supposedly) about to die – phantasms of a living person are short-lived and often seem ghostlike. Furthermore, these strange phantoms seemed to be unconsciously generated by the person whose image they are in.

For centuries, occultists, mystics and magicians have claimed to be able to project three-dimensional images of themselves and there are old Hindu texts which claim that Krishna had the ability to multiply his likeness in flesh-and-blood form. But could the average person be capable of such an incredible feat? Much of the human brain is little used and seems to be lying dormant. Could these areas be for some future stage of human evolution, when the use of telepathy and other psychic talents will become the norm? Perhaps these underused parts of the brain sometimes accidently wake up before their time and temporarily give a sneak preview of the powers the human race may one day possess. This theory would certainly throw some light on the following case of a projected phantom that was seen in Liverpool by three witnesses.

One January in the early 1990s, Angela, a 19-year-old Liverpool waitress, met Duncan, a 20-year-old Glaswegian, at a Bold Street cafe. The couple got on really well and, on 29 February, Angela proposed to Duncan. It was a leap year and the traditional date for women to propose to their lovers. Duncan laughed at Angela's forwardness and agreed to marry but, as he had hardly any money coming in from his job, said that she would have to wait a while for an engagement ring. Angela did not care; it was tongue-in-cheek anyway, their love surpassed any need for a ring.

Then Duncan received a letter from his brother in Glasgow. Their mother was seriously ill. The doctors had diagnosed a brain tumour but did not know whether it was cancerous or benign. Duncan decided he would have to go back to Glasgow for a few days but Angela was unable to accompany him because she needed her job to pay the bills. The couple had one night out before Duncan returned to Scotland. They went to a club and, as they walked home, they started to kiss passionately, ending up embracing beneath an enormous iron statue in Concert Street. By coincidence, the statue, entitled *Reconciliation*, was of two people embracing one another. Angela told Duncan to come back to Liverpool as soon as possible and started to cry. Duncan brushed away her tears, said he would miss her and that she would be on his mind all the time.

Next day, Duncan left the city for his hometown. As she worked in the cafe, Angela kept thinking about her boyfriend and the things they had said to one another. She looked forward to a letter or phonecall from him.

A week went by and he had not been in touch. Angela, concerned, went to the Central Library and scoured the Glasgow phonebook, looking for Duncan's surname and address. She telephoned immediately and Duncan's brother, Alastair, answered and seemed very evasive about his brother's whereabouts. In the end, he admitted that Duncan was depressed about his mother's condition and had drowned his sorrows in the local pub with a former girlfriend.

In a state of numb shock, Angela said, "well, tell him to get in touch with me," and walked all the way from William Brown Street to the Dingle, with a choking lump in her throat. "How could he do this to me?" she kept thinking.

Another week went by. The darkest week in her life. She could hardly eat and would not go out with her friends. Each morning she would wait in vain for the postman to see if Duncan had sent a letter. Angela's two friends, Gina and Zoe, finally persuaded their broken-hearted girlfriend to go out with them. The girls went to a club in Wood Street and had a great night. At 2.30 that morning, the girls walked up Bold Street, singing and laughing until they saw something that they would talk about for the rest of their lives.

The ghostly figure of a young man was standing at the base of the statue in Concert Street. He had his back turned to the girls, so they could not see his face. He had his head bowed, his hands resting on the statue. The girls halted in their tracks, the figure was partially transparent. Gina swore and started to run shouting, "it's a ghost!"

Zoe and Angela grabbed her and told her to calm down. They were more intrigued than frightened, but Angela almost fainted when the ghost slowly turned. It was the ghost of Duncan. He walked away from the statue and seemed to be crying.

Angela ran from her mates and rushed in her high heels over to the ghostly figure shouting, "Duncan!" Duncan did not react. He just faded away into thin air.

The girls were so shocked and frightened that none of them remembered walking to Zoe's flat in Brownlow Hill. The three of them sat up all night, each of them going over their version of the strange incident.

A few days later, Duncan walked into the cafe in Bold Street where Angela worked. She almost dropped a tray of cups when she saw him standing there with a bunch of flowers. He said his mother had been operated on, that she was well on the road to recovery now, adding that the last weeks had been a living nightmare. He denied that he had been seeing his old flame. She had just provided platonic support for him in his hour of need, that was all.

Duncan then told a strange tale. He said that the previous Friday at 2.30am, he had wandered the streets of Glasgow's city centre, when he saw an exact replica of the iron statue in Liverpool's Concert Street. Duncan had immediately thought of Angela and hugged the statue and kept picturing himself in Liverpool with his girl.

At that exact moment, Angela and her friends had seen Duncan's figure at the base of the same statue off Bold Street. Angela and Duncan had not been aware that there were three copies of the statue in Concert Street which were unveiled in Belfast, Glasgow and Liverpool at the same time, as a symbolic gesture of peace, in 1990.

# Rambling Rose

The following story has been vouched for by many people over the years and concerns a particularly gruesome apparition. Let me warn you now; if you are a security guard in the Liverpool area, look out for Rose; because you have a very good chance of seeing her … perhaps tonight.

The alarming apparition was first seen in the mid-1970s at a certain premises which security guards patrolled into the small hours. In 1975, a new guard named Trevor was walking down the corridors of this building. He was a bit nervous and kept wondering what he would do and how he would react if intruders actually got into the building he was guarding.

"What if they're armed?" he thought, as he turned a corner.

For some unfathomable reason, he expected to find someone standing there. In his mind's eye he had caught a glimpse of a woman with her arms outstretched towards him. He thought it was strange to receive such an unusual mental impression. Then Trevor felt an icy sensation creeping up his spine, knowing there was something behind him and he became gripped with fear. He gulped and walked on slowly, afraid to turn around but, as he reached the door ahead, he saw the reflection of the thing behind him – a naked woman with long matted hair and a skeletal face – reaching out towards him.

Trevor pushed the door open and ran as fast as his legs could carry him up the stairs to the next floor to where his colleague, Brian, was patrolling.

"Brian! I just saw the ghost," shouted Trevor, "it was horrible!"

"Don't talk stupid," responded Brian but then his jaw dropped, let out a terrible scream and made a scramble for an empty storeroom, with Trevor following close behind.

"Switch the light on!" Trevor yelled, as Brian located the light switch. A feeble 40-watt light bulb burned in a dusty lamp shade. The handle of the door turned twice, startling the two guards.

Trevor panicked and screamed a string of four-letter obscenities at the thing on the other side of the door. Then there was a long silence. The guards could hear the door in the other room close but Trevor and Brian did not venture out of the room until six in the morning.

"Was it that thing you were talking about the other night?" Trevor asked Brian, recalling the ghost story Brian had once told him.

Brian nodded, "yeah – Rose. The other fellow used to call her that after that old song, 'Ramblin' Rose'."

"I think I'll hand me cards in. I'm not staying on here."

"Oh nice one, leave me here on me own," stammered Brian, still shaking from the encounter.

"It was so solid. What does it look like, Brian?"

"It's a woman. She's in the nude but she's got parts of her skin missing like she's been cut up. She's got no skin on her face, just all exposed muscle and bone. Her eyeballs are the worst. One of them looked as if it was burst, like a squashed tomato. The other one just stares; no lids. Her jaw was opening as if she was trying to speak. She followed you in."

"Why don't we go and get a job somewhere else?" suggested Trevor.

Brian nodded, "I think you're right. I've been here nine months and I thought all the stories about Ramblin' Rose were just a load of old rubbish but about a month back, I kept on finding lights switched back on. Then I heard footsteps in the corridor and started seeing something out the corner of me eye. Now I know why they pay so much per hour. See, she makes one big appearance like earlier on, then she might not appear again for weeks. The last fellow who was here said she didn't appear for six months once".

"Forget all that, Brian, we'll tell the boss to shove the job," Trevor insisted.

"The money's good though, Trevor, that's the only thing. I'm up to me eyeballs in debt and Maureen would kill me if I just packed the job in. Shall we just stick it one more night and see what happens?" Brian suggested.

"No way! I'm not staying here in this place again tonight," Trevor said, shaking his head, as he re-lived the frightening experience.

"Look, if she does put in an appearance, I swear that I'll leave the building with you immediately. How's that?" Brian offered.

Trevor grumbled but, as it was getting light outside, the young guard did feel a bit more confident.

"What do you say, then?" Brian asked, "they reckon the dead can't hurt you; it's the living that harms … One more night?"

Trevor reluctantly agreed. The next morning at 3am, the guards patrolled the building with their torches, even though all the lights were on.

"Isn't it funny how the place isn't as scary as we imagined it to be yesterday morning?" Brian said.

Trevor smiled slightly, "hey, wouldn't it be funny if this Ramblin' Rose was just a cleaner trying to scare us?"

"That wasn't a cleaner the other morning, Trev."

"Let's stay off the subject. Stop talking about the supernatural."

The two started to chat about football. They were soon confident enough to patrol the building on their own and Trevor even shouted out, "come out Ramblin' Rose! Matt Monroe wants you. Ha ha!"

Brian shouted after him, "and you were going to pack the job in".

Trevor went down to the toilet and Brian decided to play a joke. He thought he would sneak in and tap on the toilet door.

He crept in and bent down to look under each of the cubicles to see which one Trevor was in. To his horror, he saw that under the door of one of the cubicles there were *four* feet: Trevor's Doc Martens and two yellowed, fungus-ravaged, bare feet with blackened toe-nails. Brian rushed out of the toilet and ran out of the building. Returning with two bemused policemen, they found Trevor unconscious on the toilet: his face twitching as if he was having a seizure. When he regained consciousness in hospital, he told a doctor that he had been in the toilet when he had suddenly seen a horrifying figure of a woman appear before him. Then he must have fainted with shock.

Trevor and Brian packed in the security guard job that day. The ghost was dormant for a few years, but appeared again briefly in 1980. It was seen irregularly throughout the 1980s and is now said to be on the prowl again. Three separate mediums have been called in by the management of the building to determine whose phantom it is. All three agreed it was the unquiet spirit of a young woman who died in the 1950s, having donated her body to medical science. However, it appears she was not actually dead but in a cataleptic coma which was mistaken for death. A student, who was stripping away her skin with a scalpel, panicked when his specimen screamed and reached for his throat and he stabbed her repeatedly in the heart and neck with the scalpel. Weeks later, when the body had been cut up into sections and dissected yet again by students, it was buried rather irreverently at a certain refuse site. This site was beneath the building where Ramblin' Rose roams the corridors.

# My Victorian Father

This is one of the most bizarre stories I have ever come across. I first heard it from a level-headed listener, who contacted me after hearing one of my stories on the radio.

Roger was a 27-year-old, sales assistant, working in an art shop on Renshaw Street, in 1965. One day, Richard, a local artist, came into the store and bought a large canvas and a couple of paintbrushes. He chatted to Roger, saying he would make an ideal model for his project because of his height and interesting profile. Roger was told that he would pose fully-clothed and, what was more, he would be paid, even though it would only be a 'few bob'.

Roger agreed and the artist gave him the address of his Huskisson Street studio, asking him to get there at eight the following evening. When Roger turned up, a young girl opened the door. She was very beautiful but was dressed quite dowdily in a black polo-neck sweater and a long pleated dark-brown dress.

"You must be Roger. My name's Virginia," she announced rather self-consciously.

Roger accompanied the girl up the stairs to an attic studio. The place was like an explosion in a paint factory and the combined aroma of turps and varnish was stifling.

Richard put down his palette and sat Roger in a chair with his legs crossed in a casual manner and started to sketch him. Virginia just looked on, smiling at the subject. By about 11 o'clock, Richard decided he had done enough and showed Roger his work. It was a fairly detailed drawing but still needed more work doing to it. Richard paid his new subject and asked him to come back the next day at the same time. Virginia escorted Roger down the flights of stairs and they left the flat together. Roger asked her where she lived and offered to walk her home.

She said she lived in Mount Street, adding, "I appreciate your offer to escort me home, but I must desist. You don't know what father is like, Roger. He simply does not allow me to become involved with men".

"That's a bit strict isn't it?" Roger laughed. "You're only young; you have a life to live."

Virginia started to sniffle and tremble, "I should have been back home at 9 o'clock. He will beat me now".

"No, he won't," said Roger, "Virginia, you're coming for a drink with me," and took the girl to a local pub called Ye Cracke.

Virginia seemed very nervous and looked about at the drinkers. She told Roger she had never been inside a pub before and had never tasted alcohol.

Roger said she should make up for lost time and plied her with drink. When they left, the girl was quite drunk and started to cry, saying her father would beat her senseless when she got home. Suddenly, a tall man wearing a short cape and a deerstalker hat came marching down Hope Street, swinging a cane as he strutted along.

"That's him," cried Virginia, terrified.

Roger pushed her into the shadows of a doorway and watched the antiquated-looking man walk by. As he walked past the young couple, they heard him say, "where can she be? What the deuce has happened to her?"

And he took a watch on a chain from his waistcoat and inspected it before walking on into the night.

Roger escorted Virginia to his basement flat near Catherine Street. He said he would sleep on the sofa and offered Virginia his bed but she asked him to sleep with her. Roger was taken aback when she stripped to her underwear, got in the bed and begged him to get in with her. Roger did not need a second invitation and was soon running his hands over her but he could not make love because she was wearing a chastity belt of some sort. Virginia said her father had the key and had fitted the belt to prevent her from losing her virginity.

Her father, she said, claimed he was 55 years old but an old woman in the street had told her she had been an admirer of him when they were both 20. That woman was now in her nineties. One day, when Virginia was rooting through her father's room while he was out of the house, she found an old sepia-toned picture of him wearing a top hat. The caption on the photograph read, 'Birkenhead, 1892'.

"Perhaps it was his father, or grandfather," Roger suggested.

Virginia said the man in the old photo had a mole on his left cheek, just like her father.

"What's your father's name?" Roger asked, his curiosity aroused.

"Robert Jones," replied Virginia and told Roger about the collection of wedding photographs, with dates ranging from 1895 to 1945, that she had also found.

"He has married seven times," Virginia said. "He married my mother just after the War. I think he's a devil, Roger. It's as if he's always been alive."

"Don't be silly," laughed Roger but Virginia's story was giving him the creeps. "He certainly acts Victorian; making you wear a bloody chastity belt. You must go to the police in the morning. I'll go with you. This is 1965 – not the Middle Ages," and he fell asleep embracing her.

When he awoke in the morning, she was nowhere to be seen. Roger went to Richard's studio in Huskisson Street and told him about Virginia and her father. Richard said he had always thought there was something weird about him but had no idea he had been cruel enough to make his daughter wear a chastity belt. He gave Roger the girl's address in Mount Street, but when Roger called, the house was unoccupied. The neighbours did not know where Mr Jones and his daughter had moved to and described Mr Jones as an eccentric, reclusive man, who used to stroll down the street pointing his walking cane at the television aerials, saying he would never have a television in his home because it was immoral.

Roger never saw Virginia again, but it was not the end of the story. In the severe winter of 1980, Roger – who was now aged 42 – was driving near Upper Parliament Street through a blizzard. He stopped at the traffic lights and happened to glance at the taxi on his right. The passenger was talking to a woman and pointing at the falling snowflakes. Roger suddenly recognised the man. It was Robert Jones, the old-fashioned father of Virginia. Roger realised, to his utter surprise, that he had not changed in the slightest in the 15 years that had elapsed since he had last seen him – and he still wore a deerstalker hat. Roger tried to follow the taxi but lost sight of it near Smithdown Road.

The mystery of Robert Jones haunted Roger for some time. Then, a few years later, he heard a local radio news story about how workmen in Duke Street had accidently drilled into a crumbling family vault on the edge of St James's Cemetery. According to the inscription on the vault door, the coffin of a Victorian surgeon, named Robert Jones, was buried within it. Roger was flabbergasted to discover that the vault contained three coffins belonging to the Jones family but that the coffin containing Robert Jones was missing. The report reckoned the missing coffin had probably sunk through the floor of the vault through subsidence but, to Roger, only one bizarre explanation fitted the facts; perhaps the sinister Robert Jones never died ... perhaps he is still alive ...

# Whispers from a Death Mask

In January 1922, a 24-year-old auburn-haired woman, Maggie, came out of the Vines public house, which still stands on the corner of Lime Street and Copperas Hill. She had arranged to meet a young man, Rex, who worked in a nearby hotel but there was no sign of him. Maggie shivered in the icy wind that blew down Lime Street, when a voice behind her asked, "looking for someone, Miss?"

Maggie spun round and saw a small man, about 5 feet 3 inches in height, standing there with a childish smile on his face. The man looked shabby and had stubble on his chin.

"Yes, my boyfriend. He said he'd be here at 8 o'clock," Maggie replied, glancing up and down the street once more.

"What's your boyfriend like?" the stranger inquired.

"He's got blond hair and he's quite tall."

"There's a fellow of that description talking to a man around the corner."

"Really?" said Maggie and looked up Copperas Hill.

"I'll show you where he is," said the man and took Maggie by the wrist along the street towards a narrow lane that used to stand near Bolton Street. As he reached the dimly-lit lane, he produced a small clasp knife, held it against Maggie's delicate neck and threatend, "don't scream or I'll cut your throat!"

He pushed her into an alleyway and committed a serious sexual assault, throughout which he ground his teeth loudly. Finally, he punched Maggie and she landed on a stack of wooden crates at the back of the pub.

After the attack, the police stepped up patrols in the area but, for a fortnight, there were no further attacks. Then, on the night of January 24, a small, middle-aged man seized a prostitute in Lord Nelson Street and, after an unsuccessful rape attempt, stole her earrings and purse before running off, laughing in a high-pitched voice as he went. Again, the police were unable to catch him. Three days later, there were two more attacks on women in Liverpool, one in Cropper Street, where a policeman gave chase to the rapist before he could assault the woman and the other, a mere 45 minutes later, in the very alley off Copperas Hill where he had first struck. During this assault, the man ground his teeth and then bit the 21 year-old victim's shoulder. He then ripped off a gold chain and locket and escaped into the night.

The police had no inkling as who the offender was, until an old lady walked into Cheapside Bridewell and said she had seen a small man with evil, shifty-looking eyes on many occasions. She was sure he was the rapist and told officers how he stared at the legs of young women walking up Lime

Street. The police sent out plain clothes detectives to patrol the street and, within hours, the little man appeared, ogling at every lady who passed him. The detectives followed him as he walked down Lime Street, stopped and took out a bunch of keys to unlock the door of one of Liverpool's famous attractions, Reynold's Waxworks.

The police grabbed the man, one Alfie Begg, a 57-year-old bachelor, who lived with his mother and worked as a temporary watchman at the wax museum. As the detectives took Begg into the waxworks, in handcuffs, Mr Begg started to cry, "I'm innocent of these crimes. It's all Deeming's doing."

"Deeming? Who's he?" one of the detectives asked.

It was really eerie down in the Chamber of Horrors. There was a clockwork-driven model of Marie Antoinette being guillotined and graphic torture scenes in a realistic mock-up of the Inquisition. What was even more gruesome, was the line of life-like heads of famous murderers from the 1840s to the present day. All the heads were actual plaster cast impressions, taken from the heads of the killers after they had been hanged. One of the heads was the death mask of one of the most notorious mass-murderers of all time, Frederick Deeming, the Birkenhead-born psychopath who had killed every member of his own family and then danced on their graves with his next victim.

Mr Begg pointed his handcuffed hands at the head of the killer and announced, "meet Mr Deeming."

The detectives looked at each other and shook their heads. The nightwatchman was obviously mentally disturbed.

Begg then addressed the death mask, "say hello to our visitors."

One of the detectives smirked: "he's not saying anything till he sees his solicitor, eh?"

Then a squeaky trembling voice said, "I hate coppers."

The detectives were naturally startled by the sound and looked about the other gruesome wax effigies, expecting to see someone hiding in the darkness, but there was no one else about.

"You'd better come with us, Mr Begg," said a policeman, feeling a bit edgy.

He hoped that Begg had a talent for ventriloquism.

"If I promise not to hurt any women again, will you leave me alone?" Mr Begg asked, childishly.

"Come along, sir," said one of the detectives, escorting him away from the rogue's gallery.

Begg started to cry and turned back to the death-mask of Frederick Deeming saying, "they're taking me away and it's all your fault, Mr Deeming! You made me do it!"

At the bridewell, Begg repeated that he was just a simple man who had been driven to crime because the murderer, Deeming, had forced him into carrying out the rapes and robberies. The clasp knife Begg had used was not his, but from one of the waxwork exhibits. Several people who had known Alfie Begg said the man was a stable, but somewhat slow person, not known for the quickness of his mind. He had no criminal record and had once rescued a dog from a frozen lake in Sefton Park. When a psychiatrist asked him about his conversations with the sinister talking head, Alfie Begg replied, "Mr Deeming's spirit said it was really scared because the Devil had found out that he had been hiding in his death mask for years."

The psychiatrist chuckled, "what will the Devil do to poor Mr Deeming's spirit, now that he's found him?"

Alfie Begg looked worried, "Mr Deeming said that Satan would claw his spirit back to Hell," adding, "I saw Satan once. He came up, out of the ground, in the Chamber of Horrors. I was scared."

"What did the Devil look like, Alfie?" asked the psychiatrist.

"Bloody horrible. I had nightmares. Satan is like a tall dark-haired man but he was surrounded by flames. All these terrible screaming voices were all around him. He said they were the damned – bad people trapped in Hell."

The psychiatrist scribbled Alfie's words down, dismissing him as a schizophrenic. Then Alfie held out his left hand and pointed to his wrist. There was a thick straight scar across it.

"The Devil touched me there and burned me. I cried and he laughed. He said he'd be back one day for Deeming and that he'd burn the place down."

Later that week, the police psychiatrist heard that Reynold's Wax Museum had been gutted by a fire of unknown origin. The psychiatrist visited the ruin of the waxworks and a fire officer took him down the steps to what remained of the Chamber of Horrors. In the grotesque mass of melted figures was one exhibit that had almost survived the previous night's mysterious inferno – the distorted head of Frederick Deeming. The heat had partially melted the head and its jaws had buckled open, making Deeming appear to cry out in agony. The psychiatrist and the fire officer were leaving the burnt-out shell when a faint voice cried out, "help me, Jesus!" They turned around but there was no one about.

Stranger still, when the psychiatrist visited Alfie Begg in a mental institution later that week and told him about the fire and Deeming's partially melted death mask, Begg replied, "I know! Mr Deeming told me. He was here last night, you see, then the Devil dragged him off to Hell."

# The Face at the Window

One of the oddest and most baffling phenomena of the 1960s and 1970s was the huge revival of mysticism and the occult. The man who was single-handedly responsible for reviving the worldwide interest in witchcraft was Gerald Gardner, who was born at Great Crosby in 1884.

Britain has a long history of witches and warlocks – from the Druids of thousands of years ago to the Pendle Hill witches. Officially, black magic was banned in Britain under the Witchcraft Act of 1753. This act was replaced in 1951 by the Fraudulent Mediums Act but, surely, no one believes in witches in today's high technology world? Yet they are still around – there is probably a local coven in your area.

In the summer of 1979, George Sidwell and Andrea King from Edge Hill went on a day trip to Blackpool, spending a fortune on the fair. Before heading home, Andrea saw a sign: 'Enter and Petra will look into your future. A genuine psychic of Romany descent.' George was superstitious and not keen on having his fortune read but Andrea persuaded him it was only a bit of harmless fun.

They entered the dimly-lit room and saw an old, white-haired woman, sitting at a table in the middle of which was a crystal ball on a stand. It appeared rather corny to George but Andrea thought it was exciting. The gypsy introduced herself as Petra and asked for three pounds.

George begrudgingly handed her the money, which she snatched and put in her belt. She then looked into the ball for what seemed like a very long time. George was just going to demand his money back, when Petra's eyes widened with surprise. Turning to Andrea she said, "someone has the evil eye on you."

"What?" Andrea quivered.

"The evil eye. It's a woman. You don't know her but she knows you. She wants something you've got," Petra rubbed her eyes, she seemed to be finding it hard to concentrate.

"What's the evil eye? What are you talking about?" Andrea asked.

George grabbed her hand, "I told you this was a bad idea. It's a load of rubbish. Let's go."

Andrea would not budge. She had to know more.

"What else can you see?" she asked anxiously.

"Another three pounds first, please," demanded Petra.

George was flabbergasted at the woman's effrontery: "Another three quid? No way, Gypsy Lee! Let's go, love."

George tugged at Andrea but she just said: "Don't spoil what's been a nice day out, George."

George let go of her hand in a huff and gave the gypsy another three pounds, muttering, "this had better be good."

Petra gazed back into the crystal globe. Suddenly she said, "hear my advice. Move to another home, far away from Liverpool."

"Is that it?" George said, shaking his head.

Petra took out a black velvet cloth and covered the crystal ball.

"That is all there is," she said, looking drained and fatigued.

George dragged Andrea out of the tent and the couple then argued all the way back to their Liverpool home, a seventh-storey flat in Entwistle Heights, a high-rise block of apartments. Two nights later, George was asleep in bed, while Andrea read a book. At exactly 1.45am, she glanced at the window and saw the face of someone looking in at her!

She screamed and shook George awake, pointing to the window – but the face had disappeared. Andrea explained what she had seen but George laughed, "Andrea, we're seven storeys up, how could anyone peep in at you? Unless it was Spiderman. You've been dreaming."

Andrea slept uneasily that night, held in George's embrace. At 4.00am, she opened her eyes only to find, to her horror, that the face was at the window again, the face of a woman grinning at her. Andrea pinched George's arm hard and he awoke with a cry of pain.

"What's up with you tonight?" but the face had vanished again and she did not tell George and feared for her own state of mind.

Two days later, Andrea decided to visit a hairdressers downtown. About 30 minutes into getting her hair done, she looked up and saw the reflection of a woman in a long black dress in the mirror. The woman's face was pale and she wore rather a lot of black eyeliner; making her appear even more sinister. Andrea recognised the face of the woman. It was the same face she had seen looking into her flat two days back. Suddenly, in the blinking of an eyelid, the woman vanished. Andrea let out a scream, startling the hairdresser, who had seen nothing strange.

Andrea then visited a spiritualist named Mrs Coombes who had been recommended to her by a friend. When she told Mrs Coombes about the supernatural woman who was stalking her, the medium seemed alarmed and said: "Oh, I don't want to get involved with this. This is over my head! I'm sorry but you must go!"

Mrs Coombes began to tremble and showed Andrea the door and Andrea was naturally a nervous wreck by now. What had frightened the medium off?

The next alarming encounter with the solid-looking phantom was in the most unexpected and almost comical location. Andrea was soaking in the bath on the following Sunday evening, reading the Echo. She happened to glance over the page of the newspaper – and there was the creepy woman in black, sitting on the toilet seat, grinning at the terrified girl in the bath.

Andrea instinctively screamed and threw the newspaper at the apparition but it vanished instantly.

Andrea became mentally and physically exhausted and very paranoid. She kept looking at the windows and expecting the woman to spring out at her every time she entered a room. George told her to see a psychiatrist, but Andrea insisted that she was not imagining things. Her odd behaviour proved too much of a strain on George and he finally left his girlfriend a week later, without leaving a forwarding address. Andrea was naturally devastated and yet, for some strange reason, she never saw the apparition of the woman in black while she was alone in the flat.

A fortnight later, she went to town to buy herself a dress and walked back home as it was a sunny day. As she passed Abercromby Square, she noticed George sprawled out on the grass, soaking up the sun, with a woman wearing sunglassses, lying beside him, holding his hand. Andrea's heart broke in two there and then. The proud part of her wanted to just walk on but instead she remained rooted to the spot for a while. She then found herself walking into the park to confront her ex-boyfriend and his new girlfriend.

"George!" Andrea shouted.

George and his girlfriend looked up at Andrea, startled.

"Andrea," said George, seemingly stuck for words.

"It didn't take you long to find someone else did it? She's a bit old for you isn't she, George?" Andrea said, sneering at the woman, who looked about ten to fifteen years older than George, "unless it's your Mum."

The woman next to George took off her sun shades. It was none other than the weird woman who had haunted Andrea and almost given her a nervous breakdown. The face at the window. The apparition that had followed her everywhere. Her stomach turned over.

"You!" she gasped.

"Yes ... go away or else."

"Or else what?" Andrea demanded, bravely.

The woman suddenly pointed to a man leaving the park and whispered something unintelligible. Without warning, the man collapsed onto the pavement. People rushed to his aid but he was already dead, as if his heart had simply given out.

The woman who had seemingly caused the accident then pointed at Andrea, accusingly, "now walk away. That's right."

Andrea suddenly felt the urge to walk away. Then something chilling happened. As she was turning around, almost against her will, she heard George say, "don't Andrea! Don't leave me."

But Andrea kept walking and did not stop until she was back home.

She never saw George or the mysterious woman again. To this day, Andrea believes that her boyfriend was not swept off his feet by a domineering older woman, but was taken from her by a modern witch. The police were naturally reluctant to get involved when she told them about the abduction and felt that her mind had been turned by her partner deserting her. All the same, George Sidwell was subsequently put on the missing persons register – he still has not been traced.

# The Caller

This creepy incident took place in Liverpool in 1995. In December of that year, a Jewish family moved into an Edwardian house in Aigburth. Karen, the youngest of the family, had just turned 15. She was very pretty and was often asked out on dates but she had her eye on Damon who lived near her new home. She often met him and chatted as they walked their dogs in the local park.

One night, Karen dialled directory enquiries and asked for Damon's phone number. She dialled his number but got an engaged tone. She tried again ten minutes later but the line was still busy. Karen wondered if Damon was chatting on the phone with some girl and, with that depressing thought, she hung up and decided to read a romantic novel in bed.

The phone rang later that night and Karen's father answered it. He shouted up to his daughter's bedroom, "Karen, you're wanted on the phone!"

Karen rushed downstairs and grabbed the receiver from her Dad.

A boy's voice said, "hello."

"Hi, who are you?"

"Jason. Is that Sarah?" said the boy.

"I'm afraid you've got the wrong number," said Karen and was ready to hang up.

Then the boy said, "I'm sorry. Hey, what's your name?"

"Why?" asked Karen suspiciously, yet excited at the thought of a strange boy talking to her.

"You know my name. What's yours?" said Jason with a laugh in his voice.

"It's Karen, if you must know. Okay? Now goodbye," said Karen, pretending she was about to hang up.

"No, wait!" Jason pleaded, "don't go, Karen, what do you look like? I know this sounds dead corny but I imagine you as a tall girl with big blue eyes and long black hair."

Karen blushed as if Jason was standing in front of her. She gave a little nervous laugh and her heart fluttered.

"Why are you laughing? Do you think I've been spying on you?" said Jason, "because I'm right aren't I? You are tall with long dark hair."

Karen bit her lip.

"Hundreds of girls have black hair and blue eyes. Anyway, hadn't you better go and ring Sarah? I take it she's your girlfriend?"

"Not any more," said Jason, gloomily.

"Why?" Karen inquired.

"We just lost touch. I moved away from the area you see, but I've moved back now."

"Who are you talking to?" interrupted Karen's father, suspiciously.

"Nobody," replied his daughter and glared at him for being so nosey.

"Was that your Dad?" Jason asked.

"Yeah. So, Jason, are you going to get back with Sarah?"

"No, not now. It's been too long. She's probably with someone else now. Listen, why don't we meet somewhere?"

"What? Meet? I don't know. I don't really know you!" said Karen, twisting the telephone flex round her fingers.

"Go on, it would be a laugh," Jason insisted.

"Karen, who is that on the phone?" her father asked.

"A friend – okay?" Karen shouted.

"Who is he?"

"His name's Jason! Can't I talk to my own friends without you asking me twenty questions?"

"Don't talk to us like that!" Karen's father warned his insolent daughter.

Jason laughed, "wow, you can't half answer back. My parents used to hit me when I gave cheek."

To get back at her parents, Karen said, "okay, I'll meet you someplace. How about McDonald's?"

"Where?" asked Jason, startled and surprised.

"You know, on the corner of Church Street and Paradise Street," said Karen, in a deliberately loud voice.

The girl's parents looked on, outraged.

"Okay, McDonald's then. What time?" Jason asked.

"After school; about 4.15 to 4.30. How will we know each other?"

"I'll be wearing a blue T-shirt and I've got blond curly hair. I'll wait for you outside, near the entrance. Anyway, I'll know you, because you're tall with long black hair, aren't you?"

"I'm not that tall, about five, seven. See you tomorrow then."

Karen hung up and went up to her room, feeling excited about the bizarre blind date.

The following day, she arrived at McDonald's at ten past four but there was no sign of Jason. He did not turn up but phoned that night to say he had got cold feet and bottled out at the last minute. So another romantic rendezvous was arranged, again at McDonald's. Jason did not show up again. This time, he said he was detained at school for messing about in class. Karen did not believe him and asked which school he attended. Jason told her that he went to Nugent High School in Edge Hill. When Karen told her Mum, she said that was strange, because her friend's son had been to the Nugent High School and it had been demolished years ago. When Jason rang again, Karen, told him he was a liar and Jason hung up after saying, "I love you, Karen and you don't know why I'm shy."

Karen felt guilty about accusing her new friend of lying and when he rang again, she said, "Jason, I really like you. I don't know why you don't want to meet me, but if you're worried I might think you're spotty, or too small or ugly, I swear I will still like you. You've got a boss personality and I think … oh nothing."

"You think what?" asked Jason.

Karen looked around and waited until her Mum went into the kitchen, then she whispered: "I love you. Now do you believe me?"

"I love you too," Jason said and started to cry.

"Don't cry," Karen said, "I don't care what you look like. We'll meet tonight? You can come around to my house."

She gave him her address and he promised he would arrive at seven that evening. Seven o'clock came and went and there was no sign of the boy.

At 9.00pm, the phone rang and Karen dashed to answer it. It was Jason and he finally dropped the bombshell.

"You won't be hearing from me again, Karen," he stammered, in a broken voice.

"Don't be stupid," Karen said, asking him why he never turned up.

"You want to know the truth?" Jason sniffled.

"Yes, get it off your chest. Tell me why you won't face me?" Karen demanded, desperate to know.

"I've been dead for five years. Dead!" Jason screamed and the line went silent – deadly silent.

That was the last Karen ever heard from the boy. Her mother got in touch with a psychic research group and they claimed that a boy named Jason had lived in Karen's Aigburth home five years before. Jason had dropped dead while playing football outside in the street because he had something wrong with his heart. Was this the same Jason who had developed a crush on Karen? The psychic investigators thought so, because they discovered that Jason had had curly blond hair and that he had been dating a girl named Sarah before his untimely death. Even now, whenever the phone rings, Karen still jumps – just in case it's him.

# The Camera Never Lies

The following strange story is a well-documented incident which took place in the late 19th century in Liverpool.

In July 1897, 56-year-old Mrs Eliza Marwood passed away at her home in Grove Street, Wavertree. In the front parlour of her house, she was laid to rest in an open coffin and covered in roses. Thick white drapes on the windows, put up as a traditional mark of respect, allowed very little light into the parlour. Mr Marwood summoned a competent photographer named Anthony Parkes to take a tasteful series of photographs of the wake but when the cameraman arrived, he said the thick curtains on the windows were not letting in sufficient light to allow him to take a photograph of the subject in the normal manner. A flash would make the corpse seem even paler.

"Then what do you propose?" asked Mr Marwood. He certainly had no intentions of opening the curtains; that would be highly disrespectful.

"I will have to take a long exposure. A series of exposures, in fact, if you wish to have several plates made."

"Very well, do what you must," said Mr Marwood and the photographer replied that he would need the utmost privacy, with no interruptions. Mr Marwood left the parlour and told the rest of the family not to enter for an hour.

Mr Parkes was a little unnerved by the task. It was the first time he had photographed a corpse, although many families who regarded the camera as a novelty were now having loved ones who had passed away photographed for posterity. He set up his camera on a tripod and, after focusing and opening the aperture to its full extent, to allow as much light into the camera as possible, he opened the shutter, uncapped the lens and stepped out of the parlour for a while. He calculated he would give the first exposure just three minutes but did not fancy hanging around the corpse in the silent parlour for even that short span of time.

"Has a problem arisen?" Mr Marwood asked the cameraman, who emerged from the parlour looking slightly anxious.

"No, sir," Mr Parkes reassured him, "I merely came out to minimise any vibration to the camera while it takes the photograph."

The photographer studied his pocket watch until the allotted time had passed.

Mr Parkes took two more exposures of the body and then returned to his darkroom in the attic of his house in Aigburth Road. By the red lamp which hung from a crossbeam in the attic, he began to develop the glass plates. He held the plate by the edges, between his fingers, and moved it about in the tray of developer. Slowly, the ghostly image of Mrs Marwood started to materialise on the plate. What Mr Parkes saw on that plate almost made him drop it with fright.

Mrs Marwood's eyes were wide open and staring with an angry, sinister look, straight into the camera lens, yet Mr Parkes had known that the eyes of the corpse had, of course, been closed while it was lying in the parlour. He put the plate in the stop tray to prevent over-development, then treated it with fixer to stabilise the image.

With trepidation, he went about developing the next plate. This picture was even more disturbing, for it showed a curious blur which looked as though it had been caused by the corpse moving its head during the long exposure. Mr Parkes knew this was impossible. The only explanation he could think of was that a small child had hidden in the parlour during the exposures and had moved the coffin – but that would not explain how the eyes were staring with such a lifelike gaze.

The third plate was finally developed and it showed what resembled a long, fine, transparent veil, hanging vertically over the open coffin. The end of this strange cobweb-like mass seemed to taper into Mrs Marwood's mouth.

Although Mr Parkes was a scientific man, he had a sneaking suspicion that the camera had somehow captured the dead woman's spirit leaving her body.

Parkes wrestled with his principles for some time, then finally decided to show the unsettling photographs to Mr Marwood.

Mr Marwood recoiled in terror when he saw the plates and accused the photographer of faking the strange effects his camera had recorded. Mr Parkes pointed out that he had not even been present during the exposures; he had been standing outside the parlour as the camera recorded the strange images.

After Mr Parkes had left, a niece of Mr Marwood came forward and said that something strange had happened when she had gone into the parlour to pay her last respects to her late aunt. The girl had been praying four feet away from the open coffin, when she had heard a sound. She opened her eyes and saw that three of the roses from the enormous bouquet on Mrs Marwood's chest, had just been hurled across the room and had landed on the lid of the piano. Then something even more startling happened – the niece swore that she saw her dead aunt open one eye for a moment then shut it again. The girl was so scared she immediately left the parlour.

What became of the weird photographic plates is unknown but they were meticulously analysed by the Psychical Research Society who could provide no explanation. However, the neighbours of the Marwood family later claimed that the ghostly goings-on at the wake were due to the fact that Mr Marwood was having an affair with the very florist who had supplied him with the floral tributes for the funeral. It is said that, even today, the house in Grove Street is still haunted by the forlorn-looking phantom of the betrayed Mrs Marwood.

# The Clock-Watcher

In 1958, a postal worker named George Jones, was out shopping with his wife, Claire, in Liverpool's Lime Street. Claire stopped in front of a jeweller's window and gazed dreamily at the array of rings and necklaces in their crimson velvet-lined trays.

"Don't start, love," moaned George.

"Ooh, isn't that ring lovely?" sighed Claire, wistfully, pointing to a gold ring with a single iridescent sapphire.

"I'm a postman, not Rockefeller," George grumbled.

Claire ignored the remark and entered the jewellers. George rolled his eyes and reluctantly followed her into the store.

"Isn't that a lovely clock?"

Claire had noticed an unusual timepiece in a glass case mounted on the top shelf. The clock had a beautiful dark blue enamel finish and an intricate stand made of cream-coloured porcelain. The clockface was framed with a golden circular band and the hours were inscribed in Roman numerals.

George looked up at the clock, then turned to the jeweller, an old grey-haired man. In a resigned voice, he asked the price.

"Twenty pounds," the jeweller replied as his wife suddenly appeared from the back of the shop, wringing her hands anxiously.

"Oh, we've got to have it, George," Claire said, tugging her husband's arm.

George realised that Claire had forgotten about the expensive-looking sapphire ring in the window, so, with a smug look, he took out his wallet and counted out the 20 pounds in notes.

"If it makes you happy, love," George said, handing the money to the jeweller.

The jeweller's wife could not contain her joy at the sale and George surmised that business was slow and assumed that was why the jeweller and his wife were so excited. The jeweller wrote out a receipt and then fetched a small ladder in order to reach the clock. He gently put it on the counter and his wife brought a cardboard box from the back room with straw and newspaper to package the timepiece.

At this point, Claire noticed an unusual feature on the clock. A little black enamelled devil was sitting on top of its case. The little horned devil was slumped forward as if he had nodded off and in his hand he clutched a three-pronged fork. Claire thought the little devil looked rather cute with his tiny pointed tail and little red cloak.

"George, look, the little devil's head moves," said Claire excitedly, suddenly noticing that the little figure's head was nodding slightly.

The jeweller laughed nervously: "That's right. It's the pendulum action.

He's supposed to be the devil having a sleep. He's nodded off, so all the evil in the world has stopped. But when the clock stops, he springs up and opens his eyes. His eyes are two tiny little green emeralds."

"Bloody weird, if you ask me," muttered George.

"A French clockmaker made a limited number of these. A Monsieur Fericul of Rouen. So this timepiece is a real investment, provided you look after it."

That afternoon, at her home in Muirhead Avenue, Claire put the new clock on the mantelpiece and invited her neighbours round to show it to them. However, she had forgotten to wind it up and slowly, the sleeping devil on top of the clock was lifting and dropping his head, as if he was ready to wake at any moment.

Claire's neighbours from next door were two old spinsters, Lily and Nellie. They sat at the table in the living room, sipping tea and nibbling sandwiches as they eyed the clock with unbridled jealousy.

"It looks stupid, Claire. Whatever made you buy it?" asked Nellie, smiling at Lily.

Lily carried her cup and saucer over to the mantelpiece and inspected the clock. She stroked the little slumbering devil and asked, "what's this supposed to be?"

At that moment, there was a strange silence. The clock had stopped ticking. The devil on top of it looked up and his eyelids opened, revealing a pair of exceedingly sinister-looking emerald eyes. Lily dropped the cup and saucer.

"Lily! You butterfingers!" said Nellie.

Lily collapsed. As she fell, her head hit the stone mantelpiece, knocking her front teeth out. The woman lay there, shaking violently with terrible spasms. Her face was contorted and twitched as if she was having a seizure. Her eyes rolled about and blood trickled down both nostrils. Nelly screamed and she and Claire went to pick up the fallen pensioner. But Lily was dead. Her sister kept shaking her and calling her name. The blood would not stop gushing out the old woman's nostrils and also began to seep out of her ears.

At the Northern General Hospital, doctors said it looked as if Lily had died of a brain haemorrhage. No one had yet connected the tragedy to the clockwork devil, waking from his slumber to cast his malevolent green gaze.

George wound up the clock and looked closely at the word inscribed on the dial. It said, 'Fericul', supposedly the name of the French clockmaker. The postman thought there was something strange about the name but he could not think what it was.

Four days later, the devil was getting restless in his sleep again, as the clock slowly wound down. George and Claire did not notice, they were watching television. Although George was engrossed in the programme, he suddenly felt an icy chill and had the feeling he was being watched. He glanced at the clock on the mantelpiece – and saw that the devil on it had awakened.

As he looked at the creepy little figure, something strange occurred. The little framed picture of the Pope, that Claire had placed next to the clock, suddenly fell off the mantelpiece and landed in the grate. It seemed to George that the picture actually jumped off the mantelpiece and, naturally, it alarmed him. He did not want to scare Claire and picked up the picture, which was cracked. The following day, Pope Pius XII died. At first, George thought it was just a very strange coincidence but he began to have grave suspicions about the devil on the clock. He told Claire about his feelings towards the little figure on the timepiece but she said he was just being superstitious and silly.

All the same, when he returned from work, George would almost continuously watch the clock, to see if the devil on it was becoming restless. Claire noticed his strange behaviour and said, "you're turning into a real clock-watcher. Stop it, it's getting on my nerves."

George decided that perhaps he was being foolish and started to watch the television and read books to pass the time, instead of gazing at the clock. Claire was probably right, he was behaving like a superstitious fool.

That Saturday, George went to the football match to see Everton play. When he returned, he noticed that the clock was missing from the mantelpiece. Claire came into the living room and said, "before you ask where the clock is, I gave it away."

"What do you mean, 'gave it away'?" George asked.

"Guess what, George?" Claire said and threw her arms around her husband.

"What?" George said, puzzled at her behaviour.

"Our Mandy and her fellow have moved into that council house in Huyton they had their eyes on. I gave her that clock for the new house. She's always liked it and you said you weren't keen on it."

"But, but," George stammered, feeling that the clock would bring bad luck to his recently-married daughter.

"But what?" Claire asked.

"Nothing," George replied but he felt uncomfortable about the clock being in his daughter's possession.

He walked out of the house and asked his friend across the road to give him a lift to his daughter's new home.

When he arrived at the terraced house, no one answered. He looked through the window into the living room and was filled with sheer panic at the scene which confronted him. Mandy's husband, Paul, was slumped on the sofa, and next to him, hanging halfway off the sofa was their mongrel dog, Sam. The dog's eyes were open, yet lifeless.

George and his friend kicked in the door and entered the living room. They were greeted by a blast of stale, warm air. Paul and the dog had died from carbon monoxide poisoning, due to a blocked flue in the gas fire. On the mantelpiece was the clock Claire had given to the couple. The devil was sitting up, looking at Paul's dead body lying on the sofa. George's daughter suddenly came in from her trip to the shop and was surprised to see her dad and his friend. Then she saw Paul lying there next to his dog and her father told her the terrible news. The girl let out a scream and broke down.

George picked up the clock and said he was going to smash it up in the alleyway but his friend Henry said he'd take the clock off his hands, telling George that he was being irrational.

Henry's family also suffered a catalogue of tragedies and Henry gradually noticed that the misfortune and grief always seemed to be triggered when the devil on top of the clock awoke. Henry sold the clock to a secondhand shop. He was glad to get rid of it.

By the way, no clockmaker named Monsieur Fericul has ever been traced in Rouen; but Fericul could just be an anagram of the Devil's old name.

# The Electrified Man

This strange incident occurred in the Broadgreen area of Liverpool and the alarming apparition mentioned in this story is still occasionally seen.

In May 1995, an elderly couple living near the train station in Broadgreen, telephoned the police after they both sighted a man standing on the track, about 600 yards down the line from the main platform. The couple said that the figure was lit up and looked as if it was being electrocuted. The elderly man fetched his binoculars and took a look at the figure and what he saw sent a shudder down his spine. A man was standing on the railway track shaking in convulsions, his mouth wide open, with bolts of electricity shooting across his body. Smoke was billowing out of the man's mouth and from parts of his legs and shoulders. About a minute into the horrifying spectacle, the man could no longer be seen and the electrical discharges ceased. The elderly man assumed that he had fallen onto the track.

When the police converged on the track, there was no sign of a body on the line and when the videotapes of the railway security cameras were replayed, there was no footage of anyone being electrocuted. Yet, less than a week later, the electrified figure was reported again, this time by passengers on a train who were disembarking at Broadgreen Station.

They told British Rail officials and the police that they had first smelt a terrible burning aroma, then had seen a man on the line, a few hundred yards away, who was lit up by flashing blue and purple bolts of electricity that surrounded his trembling body. One of the witnesses, a student from John Moores University, let out a scream and had to look away, thinking she was witnessing a man being electrocuted. Seconds later, the travellers saw that there was no man there, just a faint wisp of smoke and an acrid smell.

Two independent ghost researchers got involved in the strange case and they learned that, around the time of the sightings of the electrified man, a woman in a house overlooking the railway track, had encountered a frightening apparition in her garden at 10 o'clock one evening. She had been taking her washing off the line when her hair suddenly stood on end and crackled with what felt like static electricity. The woman felt as if the hair on the back of her head was being tugged. The woman turned around as the static tingled in her scalp and saw a man about 20 feet away, standing in her garden. The man was completely bald and wore bib-and-brace type of overalls. An aura of pale blue light surrounded him and, as he walked towards her, he grinned and reached out with his arms. As the stranger got closer, the woman felt her face tingle with electricity. She dropped the washing and turned and ran as fast as she could into her house. She slammed the door behind her and put the bolt on, before frantically telephoning her husband. A series of loud clicks came from the earpiece, so she tried to re-dial but the same interference was on the line. Then she noticed a bluish glow near her kitchen window and the bald-headed figure peering in at her. She screamed and the figure seemed startled and moved away.

The woman tried to phone her husband once again and, this time, she got through. Her husband immediately returned home. As he drove up the drive, his car stalled for no apparent reason, as if something had interfered with the engine. Curiously enough, around that time, the *Liverpool Echo* also reported that there was a lot of television interference in the Broadgreen area. Was the electrified phantom the culprit?

Over the rest of that month, the glowing figure was seen by a taxi driver, a newspaper-delivery boy and a woman who was walking her dog near the railway track. A psychic who became involved in the case said that the apparition was the ghost of a railway worker who had been electrocuted on the line in the late 1950s. He claimed that the earthbound spirit was lonely and wanted to take the life of a woman, so he would have some company.

# The Lighthouse Ghoul

Perch Rock is a large outcrop of red sandstone which juts out into the River Mersey from the northern tip of the Wirral Peninsula. The cliffs that line the coast from Perch Rock to the Dee Estuary, are known to be riddled with tunnels and caverns that were once used by smugglers and there are many fascinating old tales about this stretch of coastline; but the following story is not about contraband, it is about murder and the supernatural …

In the summer of 1827, the foundation stone of the New Brighton Lighthouse was laid in the middle of Perch Rock by the Liverpool Dock Trustees. Granite was brought from Anglesey and volcanic cement from the slopes of Mount Etna for the foundation of the lighthouse, which was opened in March 1830. The tower stood 90 feet high and the powerful beam of its light was soon sweeping Liverpool Bay to guide ships on their voyages.

The first keeper, an elderly man named Garratt, died unexpectedly at the lighthouse one night and was quickly replaced by a 65-year-old, ex-sea captain from Wallasey, Jack Maudley.

Maudley was regarded as an odd character by those who knew him. He was a loner, with a black cat which he took everywhere. Maudley wrote to his brother in Liverpool telling him of his new job, saying that he would enjoy the isolation on Perch Rock where he would be far removed from the wagging tongues of his neighbourhood. Maudley was referring to the (not entirely unfounded) rumours of him spying on young ladies with a telescope from his attic.

Mr Maudley and his faithful feline soon settled in at the lighthouse. Maudley read book after book and wrote several more letters to his brother. In one of these letters, he wrote that he missed his old house and even his confounded gossiping neighbours. He also mentioned that he was having strange dreams about making love to young ladies. Maudley's brother wrote back, telling him that his unhealthy, lecherous dreams could be prevented, if he would say his prayers to the Almighty for an hour before retiring each night.

But Maudley began a diary, recording all his innermost and perverse thoughts about having sex with an imaginary young lady. His handwriting seemed to become more jagged and angular as he wrote about his carnal cravings and, at one point in the diary, he stabbed the page repeatedly with the point of his nib.

One sunny April morning, at 11 o'clock, Maudley's heart jumped when he glanced out from the window of his quarters in the lighthouse. On the rocks below strolled a pretty girl of about 17 or 18. She wore a black straw boater and was holding up her skirt to her knees, as she carefully walked around the deep pools on the rock. Under her arm was a long cane with a fine fishnet at the end and she carried a jar to hold any fish or crabs that she caught. The girl's name was Molly Jenkins and she had ventured onto Perch Rock at low tide, the only time the rock was accessible. In a few hours, the tide would turn and the rock would we covered again by 20 feet of seawater.

It is hard for a normal person to imagine the intense, erotic turmoil Maudley must have experienced, when he first set eyes upon that young maiden on that sunny morning. What vile urges the lighthouseman felt that day will never be fully known but they must have driven him to violence, because Molly Jenkins disappeared that morning, although her black straw bonnet and fishing net were found that afternoon, drifting out with the tide.

The police asked Maudley if he had seen the missing girl and he said he had not. Yet in his secret diary, the old lighthouse keeper had sketched a girl wearing a boater with the words, "Molly I am so sorry," scrawled next to it.

On 30 July of that year, at 9 o'clock at night, Jack Maudley's 16-year-old nephew, Richard, came to the lighthouse carrying a lantern across Perch Rock. The tide was starting to come in and the boy panicked and began to hammer on the main door of the lighthouse with his fist. His Uncle Jack opened the door a few minutes later and reluctantly admitted the boy into the building.

"I've run away from home, Uncle Jack," Richard told Maudley and followed him up the long winding steps to the living quarters.

"I told them I wanted to stay with you, Uncle, and my father said you … er," the boy mumbled and could not finish the sentence.

"Your father said what?" Maudley retorted, as he halted on the steps and turned to face his nephew. His face looking sinister and distorted in the light of the lantern.

"Well, Uncle, father says you are – eccentric," Richard replied timidly and blushed.

"What else did he say? Tell me!" shouted Maudley.

"He said you are always looking at girls young enough to be your granddaughters," Richard continued.

"Hah! I couldn't give a damn what people say anymore," Maudley declared and continued to ascend the stairs.

His black cat ran down to greet its master and arched its back as it spotted Richard and turned and fled up the flight of steps. Richard and his uncle sat in the living quarters playing chess for a couple of hours, then the boy said he would love to see the powerful light up in the turret of the lighthouse, so Maudley took him up to have a look. The view from the turret was a vast panorama of blackness. Now and then, the revolving beam of light made the foam of the waves below shimmer and sparkle, but otherwise a black void encompassed the building.

At midnight, a terrible thunderstorm rolled in from the Irish Sea. Gales howled through the building and rain lashed at the windows of the turret.

Lightning streaked down from the heavens and a searing, blinding bolt came down and struck the lightning conductor on the roof. Less than a heartbeat later, a powerful thunderclap shook the foundations of the lighthouse. Mr Maudley quickly escorted his nephew down to the living quarters for safety.

Richard sat in front of the small open fire in the room and listened to the storm raging outside. Then he heard the screams. At first, he thought it was the cat, but it soon became clear that it was a human wailing and screeching and it seemed to come from somewhere outside of the lighthouse.

"Uncle Jack?" Richard opened the door and crept up the steps leading to the turret. Up in the circular room of windows, was the trembling, jibbering wreck of Jack Maudley, on all fours. The black cat was purring and rubbing its affectionate face against his arm, thinking he was playing a game. All the time, the great dazzling light in the turret turned slowly on its axis, making Maudley's shadow waltz about the room.

"Uncle?"

Maudley jumped and turned to face him with a startled look. His face was white and his eyes bulged.

"Go back downstairs!" the keeper shouted and then looked back at the rain-battered windows.

"What's wrong, Uncle?" Richard asked.

Then he saw what was wrong. Something emerged from the stormy blackness. Something grotesque and hideous. It was the decomposed body of a girl. Her face was pale green and her eyes were just black sockets. Black shiny seaweed hung from her skeletal, half-naked body. The ghoul's mouth opened wide and let out the terrible wailing sound that Richard had heard minutes before. She floated nearer and nearer to the windows of the turret, until the light swept over her rotting body.

Richard's stomach turned over and his knees felt weak. He became nauseous, yet he was transfixed by the grim sight. The ghoul looked like the mortal remains of a girl he had once had a crush on. It looked like the shell of Molly Jenkins.

Jack Maudley glanced up at the screaming vision and the terrible apparition pointed an accusing bony finger at him. The finger tapped repeatedly on the window. Then, as suddenly as it had started, the storm outside abated.

In the eerie calm, the corpse moaned, "you ... you killed me..."

In blind panic, Richard fled from the glass-lined turret and ran helter-skelter downstairs in the darkness until he reached the living quarters. He seized the lantern and raced down the winding steps.

A voice behind him screamed: "Richard, come back!"

"No!" Richard yelled, "you killed Molly! Father was right about you!"

The boy's heart pounded and he feared that his uncle would kill him too, now that he had discovered the horrible truth about Molly's mysterious disappearance.

When he reached the main door of the lighthouse, it was locked. Richard turned and saw his uncle's cat running silently down the steps out of the darkness. The cat arched its back and hissed aggressively at the boy, as it bared its pointed teeth.

Suddenly Jack Maudley loomed out of the darkness wielding a hatchet. His face had undergone a disturbing, bloodcurdling transformation and bore no resemblance to the jovial fellow who had been playing chess earlier.

"You shouldn't have come here tonight," snarled Maudley, "you should have stayed away from here. Look away," he demanded, ready to smash the teenager's skull to pieces as quickly as possible, to prevent unnecessary suffering.

"Please don't kill me, Uncle. I won't tell, I swear I won't tell," Richard pleaded.

"I know you won't tell, laddy. The dead can't speak," sneered Maudley, as he gritted his teeth and tapped his open hand with the blade of the hatchet, poised to strike.

Richard screamed, expecting to meet his doom, but then something darkly comical happened. The black cat got under Maudley's feet and the keeper fell down the last ten steps of the building. He tumbled down the steps, gashing his forehead on the final step. The evil old mariner lay there, motionless, as if dead. The hatchet fell from his hand and Richard noticed three keys tied with string to his uncle's belt. He pulled at them, but could not snap the strong yarn. So he removed the belt and slid the keys off. He tried the first key but it would not open the lock, nor would the second one; that was the key to Maudley's house. It had to be the third key. As Richard inserted it into the keyhole, a strong hand grabbed his ankle.

"Come here! You're not leaving here alive!" snarled Maudley. He had regained consciousness. His cat purred with delight.

Richard let out another scream as his uncle reached for the hatchet. The lighthouse keeper seized its handle, but seemed too unsteady to stand up, instead attempting to hack his nephew to death from where he lay. He took an angry swipe at the boy's kneecap but Richard pulled his leg away in time and the blade of the hatchet embedded itself deeply into the oaken door. As Maudley was trying to wrench the hatchet from the door, there was a pitiful moaning sound outside.

It was the ghoul – it was at the door.

Maudley was distracted by the spine-chilling sound and, at that tense moment, Richard managed to turn the key and pulled open the door. As he did so, the handle of the hatchet, stuck in the door, rammed into Maudley's eye, almost knocking him unconscious. Maudley let go of the boy's ankle and Richard ran screaming from the lighthouse and plunged into the sea. As he swam for the shore, choking with fear and the freezing saltwater, he managed to look back just once to see the ghoul entering the lighthouse. He could not be sure, but the terrified boy thought he heard a distant shrieking sound, as he thrashed about to save himself.

At first light, two detectives and five policemen arrived at Perch Rock at low tide. They found the main door of the lighthouse ajar and, on the steps, they came across the body of the keeper, Jack Maudley. There were marks on the walls where Maudley had struck out at someone with his hatchet but the police were at a loss to explain just who he had been fighting off. Stranger still, what could explain the strange rictus of death on the keeper's face? – the protruding tongue and bulging eyes which stared in terror? The detectives could see that someone had strangled the lighthouse keeper, someone with incredible strength but why had the killer left black, sinewy seaweed around Maudley's throat? There was one solitary clue at the murder scene. A small golden charm, in the form of an anchor, lay on the floor beside the throttled corpse. Detectives assumed it had probably belonged to the dead man but their enquiries failed to reach a satisfactory conclusion. Maudley's black cat was the only witness to the dramatic murder.

Richard Maudley told the detectives who had killed his insane uncle, but the law does not recognise the supernatural. Richard himself was suspected at first, but was subsequently cleared after a lengthy cross-examination. Through a strange quirk of fate, on the day of the terrible murder at the lighthouse, the badly decomposed body of Molly Jenkins was washed ashore on Perch Rock. The girl's mother and father came forward to identify her. Molly's father nodded in recognition but the dead girl's mother sobbed and said it could not be and the coroner asked her why not.

"She always wore her charm. A little gold anchor on a chain. I can't see any charm on this body."

The coroner shuddered when he heard this. He produced the little golden anchor found at the lighthouse and Molly's mother clutched it and broke down in tears.

The coroner was baffled. How did the charm end up at the lighthouse? If Maudley had killed the girl, who had strangled him? Even the warped diary of Maudley, which was later discovered at the lighthouse, with its incriminating reference to Molly, merely showed that the lighthouse keeper had an unbalanced mind – it didn't throw any light on the identity of the lighthouse strangler.

In the 1970s, New Brighton Lighthouse was sold off and refurbished. It was hired out to newly-married couples wanting somewhere unusual to spend their honeymoon. In 1973, one honeymooning couple allegedly heard an awful wailing sound, late one night, which seemed to come from the rock below. They never looked out of the windows, as they were too scared, but could it have been the tormented ghost of Molly Jenkins – the Lighthouse Ghoul?

# Forces are Moving Me

The following spate of terrifying incidents allegedly happened in the winter of 1949.

A couple and their three children moved into a crumbling old house in a street off Brownlow Hill. The couple, Mr and Mrs Warner, had lost their home in the north end of the city, five years previously, in the Blitz. They had been moving around various dwellings in the city until a relative told them about the four-bedroomed house which had just been vacated after the death of its solitary occupier; an old woman named Miriam Newrick.

The Warners had two beautiful twin daughters, Rita and Paula, who were 15 years old, and a 12-year-old son Malcolm. The family thought the old house was a considerable improvement on the dilapidated rooms they had lived in over the last five years and the children looked forward to having their own rooms and some measure of privacy at last.

Malcolm's mother tucked her son into bed on the first night in his own room. She kissed his forehead and then switched out the light. That night, Malcolm had a strange dream about spinning round and round in the darkness. He awoke in the pitch blackness at four in the morning, feeling dizzy and nauseous. He wanted to be sick and got out of bed, hitting his face against the wall with a loud smack. The noise woke the twins up in their bedroom next door. They heard their brother crying and went to see what was the matter.

"What's wrong, Malcolm?" Paula asked, then screamed as she saw the blood streaming from his nose.

Malcolm had tried to get out of bed but the bed had somehow rotated through 180 degrees. He did not realise it was facing the other way and had got up in the dark and bumped into the wall, almost breaking his nose.

When Malcolm's parents came to see what happening, they ordered the twins to get back to bed and told Malcolm to stop messing about, because he had school in the morning. Malcolm's dad put a handkerchief round his son's nose and when the bleeding had stopped, told him to get to sleep. Malcolm told them about the bed moving around on its own but his father reminded him that it was a sin to tell a lie. Malcolm finally slept and the rest of that night was uneventful.

However, the following night, about 15 minutes after Malcolm had got into bed, the twins heard a strange creaking noise coming from their brother's bedroom and went to investigate. They gently opened his bedroom door and switched on the light. What they saw sent them running, terrified, to their parent's room. The bed Malcolm was sleeping on was levitating five feet above the floor and rotating at high speed like a spinning top.

When Mr and Mrs Warner came into their son's bedroom, they saw that the bed was resting in the middle of the floor and Malcolm was talking in his sleep, in a deep demonic voice.

He started to whisper, "get out of this house or I'll break your necks".

Then the boy woke up with a startled expression and in the same weird voice he screamed, "Mum! Forces are moving me!"

The bed started to rotate again but this time the boy was thrown out by the centrifugal force as it whizzed round. The twins ran screaming out of the bedroom and fled down the stairs, while their parents picked up their boy and looked at the spinning bed in disbelief. A bundle of comics, belonging to Malcolm, suddenly flew at them from a bedside cabinet. Seconds later, the poltergeist activity stopped as mysteriously as it had started and the bed crashed to the floor.

Almost a week went by without incident then, on the following Friday night, strange whistling noises were heard coming down the chimney, as the Warners sat around the fireplace in the parlour, listening to the radio. The family huddled together, not knowing what to expect. A high-pitched voice came on the radio announcing, "hello folks".

There followed a loud knocking at the door, which made the family jump. Mr Warner looked out of the parlour window but there was no one on the doorstep – and yet the knocker continued to bang away on the front door. The racket got so bad that Mr Warner grabbed the poker from the fireside and went into the hall.

"What do you want?" he demanded.

"Are those girls coming out to play?" asked a peculiar, childlike voice.

Mr Warner suspected that some kid was playing tricks. He had probably tied a cotton thread to the knocker. Mr Warner opened the door and looked out into the snow-covered street. He examined the knocker and realised there was no string attached to it. He looked both ways and suddenly, a snowball hit him in the face, almost blinding him. As he wiped the ice and snow from his eyes, he felt something brush past him. Seconds later he heard screams. He rushed into the parlour with the poker and saw, to his horror, that something was pulling the twins off the floor by their pigtails. Their mother was holding onto them and Malcolm was hiding under the table, crying. As Mr Warner rushed forward, a lump of red-hot coal shot out of the fire and narrowly missed him. The twins continued to scream and rise up, until their feet dangled a couple of inches off the floor. Their mother was sent hurtling backwards by some invisible force, landing on the sofa. The same thing happened to Mr Warner. The poker flew from his hand and landed in the fireplace, then something pushed him backwards, so hard that he was thrown through the doorway and landed in the hall. The invisible force then let go of the twins and made a grab at Malcolm. It pulled him by his ankles from under the table and dragged him upwards so that he appeared to be doing a handstand.

Mrs Warner got in front of the hysterical twins and screamed, "in the name of Jesus! Go away!"

A gust of ice-cold wind suddenly blew through the parlour and almost extinguished the fire in the grate. Malcolm was released and fell on his back. About an hour later, a pair of woollen gloves belonging to Mrs Warner flew around the hallway. The gloves patted the faces of the twins and one glove went up one of the twins' skirts. The twin let out a scream and the gloves darted into the fire in the parlour.

A gruff voice then said, "spoilsports. I'll smother you in all in your beds tonight!"

The Warners decided there and then to move out of the wretched house and went to stay with Mr Warner's brother in Aigburth.

A psychic from a spiritualist society heard about the haunting and got permission to visit the haunted house. He said that he felt the presence of a little boy named John, who had been murdered at the house 100 years ago. No one took the psychic's claims seriously but, 12 years later, during the demolition of the house, the skeleton of a boy was found buried beneath the cellar. The body was never identified and the cause of death was never determined with any certainty, but the coroner believed that a large crack over the eye socket of the boy's skull could have been the result of a violent blow inflicted when he was alive. The coroner also estimated that the boy had died possibly 100 years before.

# The Stanley Park Apparition

This bizarre tale was briefly mentioned in a local newspaper in the 1960s and the incident was also fully investigated by a local paranormal expert and historian, Frank Wallace.

In 1966, 22-year-old Billy Lowry went to his sister's 21st birthday party in Stanley Park near Litherland. At around two in the morning, Billy left the party, slightly intoxicated, with Mona, a girl he had met there. She lived off Gorsey Lane and Billy walked her the half mile to her home, even though he lived over a mile in the other direction, at Warbreck Moor in Aintree.

Billy walked Mona to her door and kissed her goodnight. The girl embraced him passionately but her father came to the door. Mona asked him if Billy could sleep on the sofa to save him the long walk home. Her father replied that he certainly could not and that it was his lookout if he had to walk home so late. He grabbed Mona and, after pulling her into the hall, slammed the door in Billy's face and bolted it.

Billy slammed the gate as he left and embarked on the long journey home through the freezing, early morning drizzle. He decided to take a short cut down Sterrix Lane, which runs parallel to Ford Cemetery. An eerie silence in the lane made Billy walk as fast as he could. All the time he was walking, he had a strange feeling that he was being watched intensely by something. There was definitely an electric feeling of something evil lurking near him, so he started to whistle a Beatles' song. Moments later, he distinctly heard a voice close by. The voice cried out a single word. That word sounded like Billy's surname – Lowry.

"Lowry," said the raspy deep voice once again.

Billy knew it came from behind him but was so terrified, he did not dare turn around and did not stop running until he reached Boundary Road. Gasping for breath, he reluctantly looked back down Sterrix Lane. It was deserted.

He arrived at home at a quarter to three that morning and shuddered when he thought of the strange voice near the cemetery but countered his dark thoughts of the supernatural by thinking about the lovely Mona and her beautiful body and, with those pleasant thoughts, fell asleep.

The following day, Billy met Mona, as planned, at a coffee bar in Lord Street. The couple walked around the city hand in hand, kissing and cuddling and even went on a ferry trip. They ended up leaving a pub called the Abercromby Vaults, near Oxford Street, shortly before 11 o'clock that night. After buying chips in the city centre, they caught the late night bus from the Pier Head to Litherland. Mona said her father was away for the night and asked Billy to stay. He was so excited at the prospect, that he paid for a cab to take them to Gorsey Lane.

At one in the morning, just when they were getting ready to go to bed, Mona's father and uncle turned up and chased the young man out of the house. Billy had spent all his money by then and had to walk home to Warbreck Moor yet again.

This time, because he was feeling more intoxicated than usual, he did not feel the least bit apprehensive as he passed the Ford Cemetery and called out: "Come on, ghosts! Come and get me! You lot in there are probably more scared of me than I am of you!" and walked on with an arrogant swagger.

His bravado quickly evaporated when he heard that same chilling disembodied voice crying, "Lowry!"

Billy's heart skipped a beat and he turned around. At first he thought it was a balloon floating along towards him at eye level but, as it came closer, he realised it was a head; a skull-shaped apparition with an incredibly hideous face. It had bulging eyes that stared at him with pure hatred, a long pointed nose and a gaping mouth lined with jagged, yellowed teeth. There was no neck, just crimson shreds of flesh hanging from the head. The mouth moved slightly, still crying, "Lowry!"

Billy Lowry ran off in terror. He kept saying, "no! No!" as he ran but the floating, ghoulish head followed closely behind, repeating his surname.

"In the name of God, stay away from me," pleaded Billy.

The voice behind him ceased. Billy dared to glance back upon reaching the end of Sterrix Lane and noticed, to his relief, that the gruesome apparition had vanished. He then ran on with a stitch in his side, until he reached Dunnings Bridge Road.

The following morning, he told his parents about the spine-chilling head that had chased him and called out his name. Billy's parents stopped eating and looked at each other in silence. Billy was convinced that they were regarding him as a crank but Mr Lowry asked him to go over his story again.

When he had repeated his frightening account, Billy's father told him that his grandfather had accidently beheaded a workmate at a paper manufacturers up in Netherton in the 1930s. The man had been trying to fix the huge paper guillotine when George Lowry accidently pulled the wrong lever. The long blade came down and sliced the man's head clean off. The decapitated corpse was buried at the cemetery off Sterrix Lane, just next to the Ford Cemetery.

A subsequent investigation by Frank Wallace, a paranormal expert, uncovered many more witnesses who had seen a disembodied head floating about in Sterrix Lane, including two gravediggers who were chased by the apparition in 1961.

# The Invitation

The following story has been confirmed by many sources, including testimony from the victim himself. For various reasons, the names of people and places have been changed.

In Liverpool in the early 1990s, a group of property developers bought a parcel of land that was considered a desolate eyesore. A narrow, crumbling house stood at one end of the strip of land and the landlord who owned the old dwelling enthusiastically accepted a substantial but undisclosed sum from the developers.

There were two elderly people in the house, both of them in very bad health. The old house was their home and they told the landlord that they did not want to move. The landlord warned them that a surveyor had condemned the house but, when the old people said they had not seen any surveyor, the landlord alerted the social services. Days later, the people were taken into care by two social workers and put into sheltered accommodation.

Before this took place, something seemingly amusing took place. One of the old people saw the landlord talking to one of the property developers, a 42-year-old man named David.

The old woman shouted: "Where's Agatha going to live now?"

"She's not all there," the landlord whispered to the property developer.

David asked the old woman who Agatha was.

"Aggie!" she replied, "the very old woman who's lived with us for years. We asked her to move with us but she doesn't like the area where we're going to, because there's a church right on top of us".

David did not want to make a scene and felt sorry for the old and apparently confused, woman.

He knew there was no woman named Agatha at the condemned house but he said: "Don't you worry, love. Agatha can stay with me if she wants".

The landlord turned away and his shoulders shook as he tried to stifle a chuckle.

"Are you sure?" the old woman asked and smiled as she turned to face the old house, "Aggie! This man here says you can move in with him".

After a long pause, the old woman said, "she accepts your invitation, as long as you don't live near a church. She's a bit eccentric about churches you see".

That really amused the landlord.

"Aggie's eccentric?" he asked, grinning at the irony of the old woman's remark.

Something happened just then which wiped the grin off his face. The three people present heard laughter from the condemned house.

The property developer looked at the landlord with a puzzled expression, "did you hear that?"

The landlord nodded and quickly added that he had to go and pick his children up from school.

So the nightmare began. The pensioner went off to say goodbye to her old friends who lived around the corner and the developer fastened his seatbelt and drove off, feeling quite uneasy all of a sudden. He drove to his luxurious home in Maghull and, as he got out of his Mercedes, he distinctly felt something pat his bottom. He glanced around but there was no one about.

David told his wife, Emma, about the weird laughter in the house but she said he was being silly. They had dinner that evening and Emma went to visit her friend, Kay, who lived some miles away in Downholland Cross. Kay was involved in the preparations for a relative's wedding and Emma had promised to help out.

So David was alone for three hours that evening; at least he thought he was alone. He put on a classical record, opened a bottle of wine and relaxed on his Chesterfield, lost in Mozart. Half an hour later, he had fallen asleep.

Some time later, he was awoken by something pressing down on his chest. At first he thought that Emma had returned and was playing about, but when he opened his eyes, he discovered that a hideous old woman with a long hooked nose was pinning him down. He could not move. He was paralysed. He tried to speak but could only touch the roof of his mouth with his tongue, which felt dead. The old hag smiled and revealed three decaying yellowed teeth. Saliva dripped from both ends of her sickly, sagging pink lips. Her face was a mass of wrinkles and flabby jowls. Her watery eyes were yellow and red veins encircled her faded bluish-grey irises. She looked as if she was centuries old. Her claw-like hands undid a bun of greasy white hair and her locks fell down past her shoulder.

In a horrible raspy voice she cackled, "you are a fine lad".

David's heart felt as if it was going to explode. He kept trying to wake up from the nightmare but he slowly realised that this was no dream, it was really happening. The old crone licked his lips with her pink tongue, which was mottled with white warts.

"Ooh, I'll stay with you as your wife, if you desire, eh?"

David closed his eyes firmly for a few seconds then reopened them. The old hag was still there, still trying to molest him. From somewhere deep down, David managed to summon up the strength to move. He cried out and the old woman screamed back in protest. He managed to lift his arm and he took a swipe at the gruesome figure but it felt as if he was hitting a sack full of bones. Suddenly she was gone.

David got up and saw, to his horror, that the shadowy figure of the old woman was now at the other end of the lounge. She wet her fingers and began pinching the wicks of the perfumed candles, extinguishing them, one by one. He turned up the light dimmer and was able to see the weird-looking old woman in full light. She was crooked and bent over and she grinned at him – then disappeared.

He got into his Mercedes and drove frantically to his friend, Alec, who lived three miles away. Throughout the journey, the property developer continually felt something stroking his hair.

When David told Alec about being terrorised by the old hag, his friend assumed the wine had gone to his head, but David convinced him he was sober and deadly serious. Alec asked him why the ghost of an old woman would choose to pester him and David suddenly the old woman who was being forced to move from the condemned house on the purchased land and her concern for a certain, Agatha. Now it all made sense. Tongue-in-cheek, David had jokingly suggested that Agatha could move in with him.

"It is a bit of a coincidence, I suppose," admitted Alec, when he heard about the incident.

"Please believe me, Alec, that thing is demonic. How do I get rid of her?" pleaded David.

"I don't know. Tell her to pack her bags."

"How do you mean?"

"Just tell her to beat it."

David sighed and shook his head saying, "I don't think it will work. But hang on," he continued, "that woman today; she said something about Aggie not liking churches".

"I think you're having me on," Alec laughed nervously.

But David was not laughing, "Alec, have you got a Bible?"

"Don't start, David," Alec said, becoming increasingly disturbed by his friend's behaviour.

"Please, have you got a Bible?" David repeated and he scanned the large mahogany bookcase behind his friend.

"Yes, not that I ever read it. Here."

Alec pulled a large leather-bound copy of the Holy Bible from the shelf.

"I hope to God this works. I'll ring you later," David said and left.

Returning home, David sat in his lounge, watching the television. Suddenly, he saw something move out the corner of his eye. He turned and saw the old hag, cowering in the corner of the room. Emma was due back any minute, so he had to act now.

"Why don't you come here?" He asked the frightful apparition.

"Throw that blasted book away and I will!" the old woman said.

"Are you Agatha?" David asked and picked up the Bible.

"Yes. Please be rid of that book, m'dear. Go on, throw it on the fire," Agatha suggested, staring at the Bible, fearfully.

"You're not wanted in here any more. Get out of this house," David persisted, plucking up enough courage to take the book over to Agatha.

"You don't mean it! I know you enjoyed my caresses," leered the withered old crone.

"In the name of God, I order you to leave my home," David said, noticing that the apparition suddenly seemed transparent.

"I thought you loved me," Agatha went on, her voice becoming fainter.

He hurled the Bible at the grotesque vision and it vanished before the book passed through it.

David never told Emma about his supernatural ordeal but his wife was perplexed when he came home the next day with five copies of the Bible. The property developer placed the holy books in different rooms of the house and later visited the two old people he had forced into sheltered accommodation. He asked them who Agatha was, but they refused to comment. The old woman just said, "so you met her then?" and smiled, knowingly

David has not set eyes on the old hag since, but had graphic nightmares about her for over a year.

According to psychologists and psychical researchers, David's case is by no means an isolated one. For centuries, many people (mostly males) have reported being terrorised and assaulted by sinister entities like the witch that molested David. In fact, many psychologists have named the bizarre phenomenon, 'Old Hag Syndrome' and have noted that the traumatic experience of being assaulted seems quite real to the victim and usually occurs shortly before sleep, or just after the sleeper has awoken in the middle of the night. Involuntary catatonia (a sudden onset of paralysis) has been blamed but this does not explain why the victim sees and feels the presence of a hideous crone during the episodes. Furthermore, the Old Hag Syndrome is apparently on the increase ... sweet dreams.

# Kindred Spirits

This is a strange but touching story which took place in Liverpool's Dingle area in the early 1980s. The case has been investigated by a staggering number of paranormal investigators, yet has had no publicity at all – until now. It is the story of a lonely old bachelor, John Blythe.

John Blythe was born in 1907 in Aigburth. Even at an early age, John realised he could see things his four older brothers and two sisters could not see. One of his earliest memories was a smiling, kind-looking man with a long beard, rocking his cradle. Years later, when he was seven, John Blythe saw a portrait of the bearded man in his mother's bedroom and he was told that the man was his grandad who had died in 1902 – five years before John had been born.

At the age of 13, when John's schoolfriends were discovering the opposite sex, John told his puzzled mother that he had sent a love letter to the beautiful auburn-haired girl across the road. John asked his mother if she knew the girl's name. Mrs Blythe replied that there was no girl living in the house opposite, just two old brothers.

Almost every day, John would go missing for hours, and return late each night, dewy-eyed, telling his parents that he had just walked Emily home. John's intrigued parents asked the boy where he had been on his date and their blushing son told them that he had been walking hand-in-hand with Emily around the Palm House in Sefton Park. Mrs Blythe was naturally worried about her son's tales and rather than believe that he was courting a phantom, she surmised that he was just fantasising the episodes he had mentioned. However, one day, John came home in tears. He said that Emily would be going away soon, because her house was to be demolished and that she would not be able to live in the new house that would be built over the old one. Sure enough, just under a year later, the house facing John Blythe's was condemned and knocked down. John was devastated and almost starved to death as, heartbroken, he refused to eat.

Around this time, an elderly man who heard about John's so-called imaginary girlfriend, confirmed that a girl named Emily Webster once lived at the house that stood facing the Blythes' house. The girl in question hanged herself from the stairs after discovering that her fiance intended to marry another girl. It soon transpired that the love-struck teenager was infatuated – with none other than the ghost of a girl who had committed suicide at the house across the street 40 years before.

John Blythe continued to live in this world, and the next one, for the next 40 years and was often misunderstood and sneered at because of his talk about the invisible society of kindred spirits that was all around. He finally moved into a terraced house in Colebrooke Road in the Dingle area of Liverpool and, at this final residence, old John Blythe happily settled down with his family; a family of assorted ghosts, that is.

John's nephews and nieces regarded their old uncle as an eccentric but lovable soul and constantly advised him to move into sheltered accommodation. Mr Blythe said he was happy with his spirit-wife, Delia, who had departed the world of the living in 1900. The other members of Mr Blythe's adopted phantom family were Edward Goode, a refined top-hatted Victorian gentleman who was fascinated by the television set, and the telephone, and Mrs Ludwig, an old German maid who had also lived at the house in the 19th century. There were two other family members, 12-year-old twins, Thomas and Alice, but for some reason they were always moving backwards and forwards between this world and the hereafter.

John Blythe's living nephews and nieces obviously assumed that their uncle was going senile and was simply imagining his spirit family, but something took place which made everyone have second thoughts about the family of ghosts.

In March 1980, John Blythe tripped and fell down the stairs at his Dingle home. He lay unconscious at the foot of the stairs, with blood dripping from a gash to his forehead and a badly-broken arm. He most probably would have died there, if someone had not telephoned Mr Blythe's nephew, Steven.

When the young man answered his telephone on Sunday morning, an excited, well-spoken voice begged, "please send help. I beseech you to send assistance, for Mr Blythe has suffered a terrible fall at his home".

Steven did not recognise the caller's voice.

"Who is this?" he asked

"My name is Edward and I live at Mr Blythe's address. Please come at once or he will not be long for this world!"

The caller then the hung up. Steven hastily drove from his Knotty Ash home to Colebrooke Street. He hammered on the knocker but, getting no answer, he pushed back the flap of the letterbox and saw something that he was to remember for the rest of his life. A concerned-looking man in a black, outdated suit and a long top hat, was crouched over a man slumped at the foot of the steps. Steve saw that the man on the floor was his uncle. Nearby, two twins, a boy and a girl of about ten or 12 years of age, were giggling and pointing at the inert-looking Mr Blythe.

"Oi! What's going on? Open the door," shouted Steven, then stood back and waited.

When the door failed to open, Steven looked through the letterbox again and saw that the top-hatted stranger and the twins were nowhere to be seen. He backed up and charged at the door. The neighbours of the adjoining houses came out to see what the racket was about and, when they learned that Mr Blythe was unconscious, they put their weight behind the door, which finally yielded. An ambulance was called and Mr Blythe taken to hospital.

In his hospital bed, the old man asked his nephew how he had known about the fall down the stairs. Steven said that a mysterious man named Edward had telephoned him.

"He finally did it then," said Mr Blythe with a broad smile.

"Did what?" one of the old man's nieces asked.

"Mr Goode was always trying to use the telephone. He was absolutely intrigued by the workings of it but he used to hold the receiver upside down and couldn't dial properly. He must have called you."

Sadly, Mr Blythe passed away in his sleep on Christmas Eve of that year. Strangely enough, the sounds of a woman laughing were heard in his bedroom that night, when his nephews visited him. Perhaps it was Mr Blythe's spectral wife, Delia, overjoyed because her husband had crossed over to join her in the spirit world.

There is a strange epilogue to this incredible story. In 1996, one of Mr Blythe's nieces phoned up a certain medium appearing on a local radio station. She asked the psychic if there was anybody on the other side with any messages for her.

"Your Uncle John is over there. He said something about a house in the Dingle and that he's with his wife Delia and the twins".

Mr Blythe's niece was absolutely stunned by the medium's comments, particularly when he asked, "who's Edward? He keeps saying something about a telephone".

# The Deadly Looking-Glass

This is an eerie story about a haunted mirror. The tale begins in the 1960s and is continuing to the present day. The mirror involved might be the one hanging in your hall or living room, for its present whereabouts is unknown.

In 1966, a Malayan sailor was found dead at a lodging house near Paradise Street. The coroner was baffled by the seaman's death, because it seemed that he had died from traumatic shock, which is a scientific way of saying that the man had been so terrified by something, that his heart had stopped with the massive shock.

What could have scared the Malayan seaman to death? The police report was intriguing; it said that the sailor had been found sitting up straight on a dining chair – gazing at a long rectangular mirror with a look of complete horror. His eyes were bulging and his mouth was wide open. On a stool besides the dead man, were the melted remains of a candle.

An old captain from Borneo was interviewed and said that, on many of the islands of the South China Seas, there was a dangerous ritual called 'Mirror Staring'. In this ritual, the subject sat in a darkened room, at night, with a lit candle and stared into the mirror for as long as possible. Then things happened. The person would start to see that the face reflected in the mirror was no longer his own. It was the face of the devil within him.

The old Borneo mariner pleaded with the police, "please break the mirror that the man was gazing into, for it contains his trapped soul. Please shatter it, or his soul will be imprisoned in it forever".

The police, of course, thought the old captain was crazy and did not smash the mirror. Five months later, an Australian man stayed at the lodging house and moved into the room where the Malayan sailor had met his strange death. One evening, the Australian, Phil, thought he would go into town and decided to have a shave. He was staring in the mirror on the wall, applying the creamy lather to his face with a brush, when he suddenly saw a pair of dark eyes in the reflection. He assumed at first that they were a reflection of his own eyes and that the mirror was flawed, but when he moved away from the mirror to get his razor, the eyes remained where they were. Then Phil noticed an outline of a face around the eyes and thought the ghostly reflection was that of a Far-Eastern man. Phil was so frightened that he ran out of the lodging house with lather still on his face.

Many more strange images were glimpsed in that mirror by successive lodgers. In the end, the owner of the lodging house, a 30-year-old Irish-man, got a new mirror and gave the haunted looking-glass to a friend – without telling him of its mysterious reputation. The Irishman's friend was an arty type; a poet and photographer, Eric, who was into so-called mind expanding drugs. He hung the mirror in the parlour of his house in Pilgrim Street. Over the next couple of months, several of Eric's girlfriends claimed they had seen a horrible contorted face staring out of the mirror in the parlour. Eric thought the girls had been hallucinating on LSD, until early one Sunday morning, in August 1967, when Eric learned that there was indeed something sinister and evil about the mirror in the parlour.

At 3.15am, Eric returned home from the Pyramid Club with two girls, Nicole and Sandra. He had met them both in the El Cabala coffee bar in Bold Street and had then taken them for a night out at the club.

As Eric started to make a pot of coffee, Nicole commented, "coffee? Haven't you got something stronger?"

"I'm out of pot. Hey, wait till I show you this gizmo I made," Eric replied and pointed to the record player in the corner.

On the turntable there was a cardboard cylinder and inside the cylinder was the bulb of a lamp, hanging by a wire. Eric switched the bulb on, then turned on the record player. The turntable and the cylinder rotated and the light from the bulb shone through about 30 vertical slits that had been cut into the cylinder. When Eric switched off the main light, the effect was spectacular. The light shining through the slits in the spinning cylinder pulsated, causing a stunning strobe effect.

Nicole was impressed.

"Wow, groovy."

"It puts you in a psychedelic trance," said Eric.

Nicole and Sandra started to dance and, in the strobing light, they seemed to move in slow motion. The strobe made Eric feel dizzy but he continued making the coffee.

The girls then left the room to go the toilet, and Sandra remarked, "I hope he doesn't think we're all going to sleep in the same bed. He can sleep on the sofa".

Nicole laughed, "I think it'd be a laugh if we all slept together. You're a real prude, Sandra. Nothing will happen. Eric seems like a decent bloke".

The two girls then checked their make-up in the mirror and returned to the living room.

They found Eric sitting in the chair, lost in thought. Nicole went over to him and sat on his knee but Eric did not react.

"Stop messing about, Eric!" Nicole snapped, annoyed.

Eric did not even blink, he just stared at the mirror with a puzzled look on his face.

"What's wrong with him? Is he drunk?" Sandra asked, but Nicole realised that Eric was not drunk – he was dead.

She turned around to see what he had been looking at and saw a face she would remember for the rest of her life: a demonic, evil-looking man grinning at her in the mirror. She let out a scream and fell off Eric's lap. His body fell off the chair with a thud, his lifeless eyes staring at the carpet. Sandra looked at the mirror to see what Nicole was screaming at and she, too, saw the devilish face, which had now turned to grin at her. Sandra could not scream but ran out of the flat, pushing her friend aside in blind panic.

When the police arrived, they saw the record player strobe still turning and they switched it off and turned on the living room light. Of course, Nicole and Sandra's story was conveniently dismissed as a drug-induced hallucination and Eric's death was explained away as death from natural causes.

However, the detective who examined the scene of Eric's death as a matter of police routine, happened to be the same detective who had investigated the death of the Malayan sailor the year before and he instantly recognised the mirror. He could not express his thoughts about the haunted mirror but advised Eric's next-of-kin to dump it, although he could not give his reasons for the suggestion. The mirror was subsequently given to an old lady who lived next door to Eric. Within weeks, she and her husband reported seeing not one, but two, faces staring out at them from the mirror, which now hung in their bedroom; the face of a Far-Eastern man and the sad face of a young long-haired Caucasian.

# The Lost Family

The following story was briefly mentioned about ten years ago in the Lancet medical journal and has to rank as one of the strangest tales I have ever researched. It happened in Liverpool in the late 1970s. For various reasons, the people named and certain details, have been changed.

In 1978, Steve Jones, a man in his mid-40s, returned home to his family in Childwall after a hectic day at his office in the city. His 7-year-old son, Damon, greeted him with a bundle of drawings he had made for his father in school. Mr Jones patted him on the head and they entered the house, where Mrs Jones was watching the television.

Barbara was heavily pregnant and her eldest daughter, 15-year-old Emma, told her father that her mum had been having contractions. Mr Jones panicked and told Barbara to get in the car straight away, but his wife claimed Emma was talking nonsense; she had only had a slight cramp in her leg, that was all.

The family had settled down to tea when, suddenly, Mrs Jones stood up and announced, "Steve – I think it's time!"

Steve jumped up, almost knocking the table over, and within a minute they were in their car, heading towards Oxford Street Maternity Hospital. It was a real nightmare; the contractions were getting worse by the minute even though the baby was not supposed to be due for almost a month.

At the Fiveways roundabout, the couple's car was hit by a lorry, which pulled out in front of them. The impact sent the car rolling end over, on its roof, for about 60 yards.

Steve screamed when he realised that his heavily pregnant wife seemed lifeless. Blood trickled from her forehead and it looked as if her neck was broken. The last thing he saw before he blacked out, was an upside-down face peering into the smashed-up car.

Steve regained consciousness just over a day later in Walton Hospital's neurological department, where he had undergone emergency brain surgery to remove impacted skull fragments. The surgeon shone a light into the patient's eyes and asked him who he was.

"My name is Steve Jones," he answered groggily.

Then his thoughts turned to his wife and her unborn child, "where's my wife? Where's Barbara?"

The surgeon told him everything was fine and advised him to rest. Outside in the corridor sat Bob Jones, Steve's older brother. As the surgeon came out of the ward, Bob confronted him and asked about his brother's condition.

"He was asking how is wife, Barbara, was."

Bob looked puzzled: "But he isn't married. As far as I know he isn't even going out with anyone called Barbara".

The mystery of the missing wife deepened as Steven gradually started to recover. Bob listened at the foot of his bed as his brother told him of the events leading up to the crash at the Fiveways roundabout.

Bob thought that his brother was just confused with the head injuries and told him he was disorientated.

"Steve. You're a bachelor. You've got no family."

Steven sat up, aghast at his brother's assertion.

"What's going on, Bob? Are you trying to tell me I don't have a family? Why are you saying this? Is it a way of telling me that Barbara's dead? She didn't survive the crash, did she?"

Bob sighed and looked down at his hands.

"You're just a bit confused. Don't worry."

Steve got out of bed.

"That's it, I'm signing myself out."

Bob had to wrestle to get his irate brother back into bed. A nurse heard the shouting and came running in with an orderly.

Steve asked for a phone to be brought to his bedside and one was brought and plugged in by his bed.

"You'll see who's confused," Steve snapped, as he dialled his home number. He pictured Emma reaching for the phone. She would prove he was not imagining things. "Come on, Emma, answer the phone," he muttered, as the nurses and Bob looked on with sympathetic expressions.

He gripped the receiver tightly but the phone just kept on ringing at the other end – no one answered it.

"They must be at school; what time is it?"

"It's Saturday, Steve," Bob answered, shaking his head in despair.

"Look, please believe me. I have a wife, a daughter named Emma and a seven-year-old son named Damon. Please send someone to fetch them. Call Emma's school, please. Better still, I'll phone one of the neighbours." Steven said in desperation.

He put the receiver down, then lifted it and dialled again. Almost immediately, elderly neighbour, Mrs Steele, answered.

"Mrs Steele? It's me, Steve Jones!"

"How are you, Steve? I read about the crash in the newspaper. I called the hospital the other day but they said you were critical."

Steve interrupted impatiently.

"Mrs Steele, could you just confirm something? I know this is going to sound nuts but could you tell me that I have a family?"

There was a pause, then the bemused old lady said, "of course you have a family".

"Yes! I told them, but they wouldn't believe me. Please tell me how many there are in my family."

"Well, there's you, of course, and your brother Bob and …"

"No, Mrs Steele, not my brothers and parents; my own family – Damon and Emma."

There was a long silence before Mrs Steele replied, "I thought you didn't have a family, Steve".

"Yes, you know I have a wife and kids. You gave Damon some toffees the other day, remember?"

Mrs Steele was confused: "I'm sorry Steve but you are not making much sense. Damon? Who's Damon?"

"What are you all playing at? Is this supposed to be some kind of joke?"

Feeling threatened, Mrs Steele replied that there was someone at the door and hung up.

The surgeon came into the room and quizzed Steve about his non-existent family and assured him that his memory would soon return. Steve insisted that he was not suffering from amnesia and demanded to be allowed to return home so that he could prove his claims. The surgeon answered that it would be out of the question for at least a fortnight. However, he did allow Steve to keep the phone at his bedside. At 6 o'clock that evening, something quite bizarre happened. A young girl came into the room and gently stroked Steve's face. He awoke to her touch and saw to his great surprise that it was his daughter Emma, holding a big bouquet of flowers.

"Emma! Where's your mum?" Steve asked, reassured at the sight of his daughter.

Emma hugged him and kissed him: "What's that big bandage on your head for Dad?"

"Never mind me, where's your Mum?" Steve asked, clutching his daughter's hands tightly.

"She's in hospital. She's had the baby, hasn't she?"

"But – I thought she was – I'm so confused," Steve cried.

"You know she's in hospital," Emma said, going to the foot of the bed to study her father's progress chart.

"Was it a boy or a girl?" Steven asked, immensely relieved that the nightmare was over, hoping he had dreamt the whole episode about his brother and the nurses doubting that his family existed.

"Stop acting soft, Dad! You were at the birth. You passed out during the Caesarian and hit your head on the bed."

The door opened slightly and someone called, "Emma Jones? Here a moment, please".

As Emma walked out of the ward, Steve got out of bed and hobbled after her. He opened the door of the room and saw that the long corridor outside was empty. Deeply shocked, he felt unsteady and leaned against the wall. As a nurse came hurrying to his aid, Steve blacked out.

At 10 o'clock that night, he regained consciousness. The surgeon was shining a penlight into his eye and asking him his name.

"Steve Jones. And I know I'm in the neuro-ward. She came here today. I wasn't imagining it."

"Who came, Mr Jones?"

"Emma did," replied Steve angrily, pushing the penlight from his face and sitting upright in bed.

He pointed to the bouquet of flowers lying on the bedside cabinet: "Look! Did I imagine them?"

"Your brother left them, didn't he?" a nurse said.

"No, he didn't!" yelled Steve, "ask him if you want. Emma brought them in".

The nurse shrugged but then noticed the card pinned to the flowers with the message: 'Get well Dad. Love from Mum, Emma and Damon'.

When Steve was eventually discharged, he returned home with his brother and found the house in Childwall just as he remembered it, but with no traces of his family. Emma's bedroom was empty, as was Damon's room. In his own bedroom, there was no evidence whatsoever to prove that his wife had ever been there. No make-up, no wardrobe crammed with her clothes, nothing. A telephone inquiry to the vicar who had married Steve and Barbara Jones was treated as a crank call. Steve stormed into a house where Barbara's parents were supposed to live, but the old couple who lived there said that they did not know of any Barbara. Nor had the local schools heard of Damon, or Emma Jones.

Not surprisingly, Mr Jones underwent psychiatric observation and finally moved from Liverpool, because it held too many memories for him; memories of a happy family which had apparently been erased from reality.

If we can discount amnesia and brain injury, how can we explain Mr Jones's traumatic experience? How can we explain the bouquet left by Emma with the handwritten note? Perhaps Mr Jones was transferred after the crash from some parallel world which runs alongside our one. In this world, did Mr Jones did have the family he spoke of? For all we know, there may now be some other version of you, the reader, in this parallel world, perhaps living some entirely different life with another partner ... perhaps we will know more one day.

# Don't Look Under the Bed

This story took place in 1965 and was related to me by the two people featured in the tale, Muriel and Kenny, who now live in Wallasey. If you're reading this story in bed – don't have nightmares.

At 1.30 in the morning, Muriel and Kenny left the Mardi Gras nightclub in Mount Pleasant. They were both in their early 20s and deeply in love with each other. The only trouble was that Kenny's parents hated Muriel's parents and vice versa, so the couple had moved out of their homes in Kensington to live together in a boarding house off Liverpool's Oxford Street.

Kenny and Muriel arrived at the lodging house at about ten to two and had to sneak up to their bedsit so they would not wake up Hilda, their old landlady. Once in their room, Muriel got into bed and Kenny put the kettle on the one-ring gas stove to make a cup of tea. Muriel lit up a cigarette and relaxed in the old but sturdy double bed. Kenny made the tea, then said he had to go the toilet, so he crept out the room and sneaked down to the outside loo, which was situated in the back yard.

Muriel, meanwhile, was thinking about the great night she had just had. Muriel, who worked in John Collier's department store, would be getting her wage packet tomorrow and that meant another night out with Kenny at the Basement Club or Reeces Ballroom. As Muriel puffed on her cigarette, she was startled by a strange sound in the room. The noise sounded asthmatic – like a cough. Suddenly, she heard someone – or something – make a hooting sound. It sounded like someone saying, "ooh".

Muriel prayed for Kenny to hurry back to the bedsit. In the tense silence, she clearly heard a quivering voice say, "oh, Mother of God, no!" That was enough. She jumped off the bed as if it was on fire and ran out of the room, almost falling head first down the stairs in blind panic. She met Kenny coming up and she told him about the voice in their room.

"Don't be soft, Muriel. It's the landlady talking in her sleep. These walls are paper-thin. Come on, I'm dead beat."

"But it sounded as if it was ..." Muriel could not finish the sentence.

"Sounded as if it was what?" Kenny asked.

"Nothing," replied Muriel, enigmatically, as she climbed the stairs, clutching Kenny's hand.

"Go on," persisted an intrigued Kenny, "it sounded as if it was what?"

Muriel squeezed Kenny's hand tightly as they ascended the stairs.

"It sounded as if it was under the bed, Kenny."

A voice behind them shouted, "oi!"

Muriel and Kenny jumped with fright but it was only Hilda, wearing a funny-looking hair-net and a long gold lamé nightgown. The landlady had bloodshot eyes and looked furious.

"Do you two know it's gone two o'clock in the morning? The bloody bolt's going on at twelve o'clock next time, I'm telling you!" she snapped and disappeared back into her bedroom, slamming the door shut.

Kenny and Muriel grinned at each other and went back to their room.

"She looked like Joan Crawford in that nightgown," Kenny joked, and Muriel had to stifle a laugh.

They had a cup of tea, went to bed and fell fast asleep.

At four in the morning, something awakened Muriel. It was a faint, creepy, whispering voice, like someone saying a prayer, followed by the faint sounds of sobbing. Muriel's heart fluttered with fear. She shook Kenny awake. He heard the sound too and sat up in bed. Suddenly, something thumped the underside of the mattress.

Muriel trembled and, with a dry throat, she whispered, "it's under the bed, Kenny".

"Don't be soft, Muriel. It sounds like someone's got a radio on in the distance somewhere."

Then he, too, felt the thump underneath him. He was more intrigued than scared and reached out for his cigarette lighter and flicked it on.

He then got out of bed, bent down, looked under the bed and jokingly said, "there's a bogeyman here".

Then Kenny went pale and he let out a scream. He ran out the room and dropped the lighter, leaving Muriel in the pitch-black bedsit. Muriel, terrified, got out of bed and searched frantically for the door.

Then she heard a voice crying, "no! No! Please don't hurt me!"

Almost fainting with fear, she found the door at last and ran down the stairs. At the bottom, she fell over Kenny, who had fallen down the last two steps and was lying there, dazed. Hilda came out and switched on the landing light. She was absolutely furious and promised her noisy lodgers that they would be evicted in the morning but Kenny and Muriel left the lodging house 15 minutes later and stayed in Muriel's aunt's place in Arundel Avenue. Kenny said he had seen an old woman covered in blood with staring eyes under the bed.

A month later, in the Pink Parrot Club, a Merchant Navy seaman who had once stayed in the Oxford Street lodging house, several years back, told Kenny and Muriel the story behind the haunted bed. He said that, at the turn of the century, an escaped convict from Kirkdale Gaol had broken into an old woman's house in Aigburth and had stabbed her to death as she lay hiding under her bed. The murderer then escaped with her savings and was never caught. The niece of the old woman was Hilda, the landlady of the Oxford Street lodging house and she inherited the bed. Many people, over the years, had sworn that they had heard the old woman's final pleas being whispered under that bed, but Hilda was too mean to get rid of it.

In 1969, Hilda, the landlady, died and the whispering bed was sold to a certain second-hand furniture store in Liverpool. Could it be the very same bed you are sleeping in tonight?

# The Returned Man

This is a bizarre story, yet it was witnessed by nine people in broad daylight in the middle of Liverpool in the 1960s. The incident was investigated by Dr Ivan Hunter, the late Cambridge professor of psychology who systematically studied alleged mediums and psychics.

The story unfolded in 1968, when a couple in their 40s were leaving the Swan Pub in Liverpool's Wood Street. As Joan and Frank walked up the street, Frank told his wife he loved her, then fell down dead in the road from a massive coronary. Joan sat in the road cradling her husband, sobbing, surrounded by bystanders. An ambulance turned up but the medics could not help; Frank was dead and they could do nothing to bring him back.

After the funeral, Joan went into a terrible depression that seemed to have no end. Every evening, for over six months, she walked aimlessly around Kirkby, dressed in black, with her head bowed. She visited all the places she used to go with her late husband; the bingo, the Peacock Pub, the park where they strolled hand in hand in the summer. She even went to look at the old bus shelter where she had first told Frank that she was pregnant.

One bright summer morning, Joan's four sons and their wives and girlfriends turned up at her home with flowers, chocolates and gifts to cheer their mother up. They persuaded her to visit Liverpool city centre to do some shopping with them. Reluctantly, Joan got ready and one of her sons, Michael, drove her to town, followed by the others.

The shopping trip was going well, until Joan saw a young couple in Church Street, who looked exactly like a young version of herself and her late husband. The couple were walking along, hand in hand, smiling at each other. Joan dropped the bag and started to cry. Her sons surrounded her and comforted her.

Joan broke down, "I can't go on without him. They say it gets better as time goes on, but I can't take it any more. I wish I was with him, I really do".

A bald, distinguished-looking man, wearing sunglasses, came forward. He was dressed in a finely-cut dark blue suit and spoke in a reassuring voice.

"Excuse me," he said to Joan's sons and moved through them and their wives until he reached the bewildered Joan.

The stranger put his arm around Joan's shoulder and produced a neatly folded handkerchief.

"Here, have a good blow," he said and, turning to her sons added, "look, I know your mother. Can I just talk to her in private for a moment?" He then took Joan over to the window of a jewellers and said, "look, Joan, Frank is beside himself with grief because of the way you're behaving. You're like a little child".

Joan was confused by the his words: "What? Are you some sort of psychic?"

The man smiled, "if you knew what I was, you'd run a mile. Now, if I could convince you Frank is okay, would you promise not to go on crying all the time and being a downright misery?"

Joan nodded, wondering if the man was some religious crank or a confidence trickster.

"You haven't said you promise," continued the man.

"I promise," Joan sobbed, wiping away her tears.

The man pointed towards a tailor's shop, near the corner of Whitechapel and Church Street. There stood Frank. He nodded, smiling at Joan and laughing in reaction to the way his wife's jaw dropped.

"Frank! Frank!" shouted Joan and thrust her arms out towards the familiar figure at the end of the street.

As she started to walk towards him, the stranger held her back, saying, "you can't, Joan".

By now, one of Joan's sons, Michael, had also seen the vision of his father on the corner and Frank waved to him and gave him the thumbs up. Michael was understandably shocked and told his brothers and his wife to look – they too saw the figure. Michael shouted, "Dad!" and fought through the crowds to get to him but when he reached the corner, Frank was nowhere to be seen. His brothers, their wives and girlfriends following behind, were all in a state of total confusion. When they returned to Joan, she was alone, the stranger had left.

From that day onwards, Joan started to rebuild her life and stopped wearing black. She changed into an outgoing woman overnight and told her sons that she now knew Frank was still around. She felt as if he was literally just around some corner and that there was nothing to grieve over.

Professor Hunter interviewed all the witnesses at length and surmised that they had all collectively hallucinated an apparition of Frank but he admitted there was something strange about the case. The professor sought out the jeweller in the street where the incident had happened and the jeweller said he remembered the man in the blue suit who had comforted Joan, although he had never seen him before and had not seen him since.

Joan went on record as saying that she thought the man in the blue suit was some sort of angel who had been sent by a higher authority to give a message of hope. The whole case remains baffling and Joan herself has since died. Perhaps she is with Frank now, wherever that might be.

# Other titles by Tom Slemen

| | | |
|---|---|---|
| HAUNTED LIVERPOOL 2 | Tom Slemen | £5.99 |
| HAUNTED LIVERPOOL 3 | Tom Slemen | £5.99 |
| HAUNTED LIVERPOOL 4 | Tom Slemen | £5.99 |
| HAUNTED LIVERPOOL 5 | Tom Slemen | £5.99 |
| HAUNTED LIVERPOOL 6 | Tom Slemen | £5.99 |
| HAUNTED LIVERPOOL 7 | Tom Slemen | £5.99 |
| HAUNTED LIVERPOOL 8 | Tom Slemen | £5.99 |
| HAUNTED LIVERPOOL 9 | Tom Slemen | £5.99 |
| HAUNTED LIVERPOOL 10 | Tom Slemen | £5.99 |
| HAUNTED LIVERPOOL 11 | Tom Slemen | £5.99 |
| HAUNTED LIVERPOOL 12 | Tom Slemen | £5.99 |
| HAUNTED LIVERPOOL 13 | Tom Slemen | £5.99 |
| HAUNTED LIVERPOOL ANTHOLOGY | Tom Slemen | £6.99 |
| HAUNTED WIRRAL | Tom Slemen | £5.99 |
| STRANGE LIVERPOOL | Tom Slemen | £5.99 |
| LIVERPOOL GHOST WALK | Tom Slemen | £5.99 |
| HAUNTED CHESHIRE | Tom Slemen | £5.99 |
| WICKED LIVERPOOL | Tom Slemen | £5.99 |
| HAUNTED LIVERPOOL double cassette and audio book read by | Tom Slemen | £8.99 |

Available from all good bookshops. For a free stocklist contact:

The Bluecoat Press
19 Rodney Street
Liverpool L1 9EF

Telephone: 0151 707 2390
Website: www.bluecoatpress.co.uk

If you have had a paranormal encounter, or a supernatural experience of any sort, please drop a line to Tom Slemen c/o the above address.